Editor: Maryanne Blacker

Design Director: Neil Carlyle

∎ ∎ ∎

Assistant Editor: Judy Newman

Designer: Robbylee Phelan

Sub-editor: Danielle Farah

Cadet Artist: Louise McGeachie

Secretary: Wendy Moore

∎ ∎ ∎

Cover Photograph: Jon Bader

Cover Stylist: Marie-Helene Clauzon

∎ ∎ ∎

Illustrators: Diane Bradley, Sue Ninham

∎ ∎ ∎

Publisher: Richard Walsh

Deputy Publisher: Graham Lawrence

∎ ∎ ∎

Produced by The Australian Women's Weekly
Home Library
Typeset by Letter Perfect, Sydney.
Printed by Dai Nippon Co Ltd, Tokyo, Japan
Published by Australian Consolidated Press,
54 Park Street Sydney
Distributed by Network Distribution Company,
54 Park Street Sydney
Distributed in the U.K. by Australian Consolidated Press (UK)
Ltd (0604) 760 456.   Distributed in Canada by Whitecap
Books Ltd (604) 980 9852. Distributed in South Africa by
Intermag (011) 493 3200.

∎ ∎ ∎

Book of Gifts.
   Includes index.
   ISBN 0 949128 25 2.
   1. Gifts. 2. Handicraft. (Series : Australian
   Women's Weekly Home Library).
745.5

COVER: A selection of gifts from the book.
OPPOSITE: How Utterly Romantic, page 101.

The most memorable gifts are not necessarily the most expensive ones – those which have a lot of thought and effort wrapped up with them are often the most appreciated. Our collection of wonderful gift ideas is sure to please – you can cook, grow, stitch or paint a perfect present, swathe it in paper, fabric, ribbons or a simple bow and attach a handmade card. Delightful. Try, also, a theme gift – just the ticket for the person who has everything – buy the goodies and package them with pizazz. We show you just how easy it is to create, wrap and give a great gift!

Made by Jan Evans

MADE TO GIVE

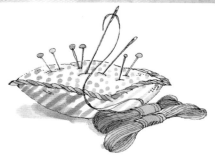

A handmade gift is always treasured; the cost is often minimal, but time and a little effort make a very special present. For best results, choose quality materials and consider colour carefully. And finally, whether you've made an heirloom toy or a handmade book, make sure it's packaged beautifully.

Heirloom Church Doll

Traditionally this delicate, embroidered doll was given to a child to take to church.

40cm square of cotton voile fabric
90cm x 15mm-wide double-edge lace (for skirt insertion)
90cm x 6cm-wide single-edge lace (for skirt hem)
30cm x 4cm-wide single-edge lace (for cape)
15cm x 4cm-wide single-edge lace (for bonnet)
50cm narrow cream silk ribbon
50cm narrow apricot silk ribbon
Six stranded embroidery thread in colours of your choice
Polyester fibre filling
Water-soluble pen
Tissue paper
Thread

Sew a 5mm hem around the fabric using hemstitch. See page 124 for stitch instructions.

Mark eye and lace positions on fabric with water-soluble pen. See diagram at right.

Cut 56cm and 25cm lengths of insertion lace. Pin and stitch 25cm length of lace onto fabric to make centre scallop at skirt hem, stitching upper edge of lace only. Pin and stitch 56cm length of lace onto fabric, stitching upper edge of lace only at either side of centre scallop,

and both edges of lace at inverted V above centre scallop.

Carefully cut away fabric from behind both lace strips. Pin a 5cm-wide strip of tissue paper to lower edge of lace along bottom of skirt, following the curves.

Gather 6cm-wide lace and pin it onto tissue paper 3mm from the edge of insertion lace. Stitch gathered lace to insertion lace using trellis stitch.

Embroider floral design on doll's skirt using stitches indicated on diagram at right. Use two strands of thread for all embroidery and work in colours of your choice.

Work one cross-stitch for each doll's eye marked on pattern. Work satin stitch to make a tiny round mouth, and French knots for hair. Embroider ringlets by working 4 parallel bullion stitches.

Cut and tie apricot silk ribbon into 2 tiny bows; stitch above ringlets.

Place a small ball of polyester fibre filling behind face to form head and secure by tying a thread firmly around the doll's neck.

Stitch 4cm-wide lace for bonnet around doll's face, gathering one edge of lace at the back of head and stitching each end under.

Gather and stitch 4cm-wide lace for cape around neck, stitching ends together at back of head. Tie cream silk ribbon into a bow and stitch to lace at front neck.

Tie the top corners of fabric into loose knots to form hands.

LEFT: Heirloom Church Doll.

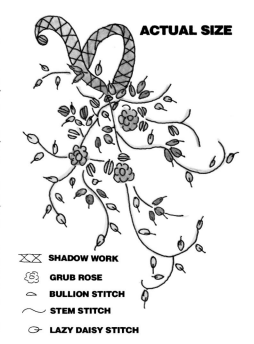

ACTUAL SIZE

XX **SHADOW WORK**
🌸 **GRUB ROSE**
⌒ **BULLION STITCH**
〜 **STEM STITCH**
🖛 **LAZY DAISY STITCH**
🥚 **SATIN STITCH**

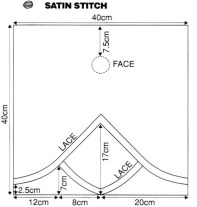

Pansy Tea-Set

TEA-COSY

64cm x 22cm fine evenweave linen
    fabric
30cm x 90cm-wide lining fabric
30cm polyester wadding
Six stranded embroidery thread (see
    key for colours)
Tapestry needle
Thread

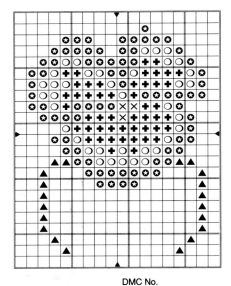

	DMC No.
✕ Yellow	725
▲ Green	320
○ Pale pink	3609 or Lilac 211
✪ Pink	3607 or Mauve 209
✚ Magenta	917 or Purple 552

Note. Work stems on left or right side
as desired.

Size: 30cm x 20cm

Following diagram below, cut 2 pieces of linen, curving top edge as shown. Zig-zag stitch edges to prevent fraying.

Using 2 strands of embroidery thread, work cross-stitch pansies on both pieces in desired positions, following graph at left. (We worked pansies in two colour combinations.) See page 124 for embroidery stitch instructions.

Cut 2 pieces of lining, same size as linen pieces. Place one linen piece over one lining piece, right sides together. Stitch along straight edge using 1cm seam allowance. Fold lining over to right side, press lining. This will form tea-cosy front.

Repeat with remaining pieces of linen and lining for tea-cosy back.

Cut two pieces of wadding same size as linen. Position a piece of wadding between linen and lining of both front and back. Tack linen, wadding and lining together around curved edge on both pieces. Place front and back right sides together; stitch curved edge using 1cm seam allowance. Turn right side out.

NAPKIN

40cm square fine evenweave linen
    fabric (for each napkin)
Six stranded embroidery thread (see
    key for colours)
Tapestry needle
Thread

Size: 38cm square

Turn under a 5mm hem around napkin, then another 5mm.

Hemstitch around napkin, pulling stitches firmly.

Using 2 strands of embroidery thread, work motif in cross-stitch in corner, following graph at left. See page 124 for stitch instructions.

TRAY CLOTH

46cm x 35cm fine evenweave linen
    fabric
Six stranded embroidery thread (see
    key for colours)
Tapestry needle
Thread

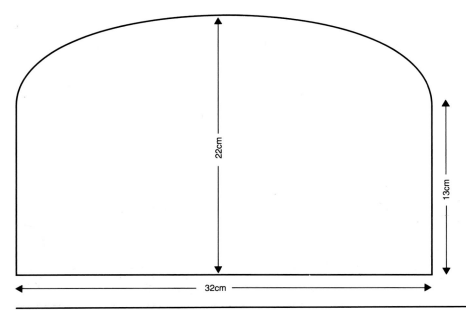

Size: 44cm x 33cm

Turn under 5mm around tray cloth, then turn another 5mm to make hem.

Hemstitch around tray cloth, pulling stitches firmly. Using 2 strands of embroidery thread, work 2 pansy motifs in cross-stitch, following graph at left. See page 124 for embroidery stitch instructions.

BELOW: Pansy Tea-Set.
Tray, vase, cushion, table: Mosmania

Made by Jan Evans

Sewing Chatelaine

2 x 10cm x 90cm-wide lightweight
   cotton print fabrics
8cm x 6cm flannel or felt
7 beads with large hole
Six stranded embroidery thread in
   3 colours to match fabric
Silk embroidery ribbon in 3 colours
   to match fabric
DMC Perle thread or 1.1m narrow
   cord
Polyester fibre filling
Embroidery scissors (for chatelaine)
Water-soluble pen

NEEDLEBOOK

Cut 2 x 12cm x 9cm rectangles, one
from each print fabric.

Place print fabric pieces right sides
together and stitch around three sides
using a 1cm seam allowance. Trim
seam and turn right side out. Turn in
remaining 1cm seam allowance and
handstitch seam closed.

Trim flannel or felt edges with pinking shears (the flannel or felt rectangle
will form needlebook pages). Fold in
half and handstitch folded edge inside
spine of book.

Using water-soluble pen, transfer
the letter of your choice onto needlebook cover. See actual size letter
diagrams below.

Work design using two strands of
embroidery thread in colour of your
choice. See page 124 for embroidery
stitch instructions. Work the letter in
satin stitch. Surround it with French
knots and star stitch, and add more
French knots using silk ribbon in
colours of your choice.

Work chain-stitch along top and bottom edges of the needlebook front using
a single strand of embroidery thread in
colour of your choice.

ACTUAL SIZE

Made by Rosa Alonso

Stitch a bead halfway along edge of book. Work a buttonhole stitch loop on the opposite edge making it long enough to fit around bead.

PIN CUSHION
Cut 2 x 7cm squares, one from each print fabric.

Pin and stitch fabric, right sides together, using a 1cm seam allowance and leaving an opening on one side. Turn through to right side. Place fibre filling inside pin cushion and stitch opening closed.

Work embroidery as for needlebook, referring to picture above, and positioning letter diagonally on pin cushion.

Work chain-stitch around edge of pin cushion using a single strand of thread in colour of your choice.

To assemble. Take 1.1m of twisted thread cord (see instructions at right) or purchased cord. Take one end of cord through loop of scissors, measure 24cm

along cord, knot end at this point so that 12cm of cord is doubled.

Thread other end of cord through 3 beads. Slip-stitch pin cushion to cord, positioning it 55cm from scissors and diagonally. Thread 3 more beads onto cord and slip-stitch needlebook spine onto cord, 15cm from pin cushion.

Make tassel (see instructions below) and stitch onto end of cord.

Twisted thread cord. Take a length of Perle thread, 3 times the desired length of the finished cord. Attach one end to work table with adhesive tape and twist in one direction. When twists appear along length of cord, pick up thread at its centre. Thread should twist around itself, making a cord.

Tassel. Wind Perle thread around 3 fingers or a piece of cardboard until it is as thick as desired. Secure by tying thread through loops at top of tassel.

Wind a length of thread around tassel near top to form neck of tassel, and

tie (diagram A). Cut through threads at base of tassel.

To decorate tassel, work buttonhole stitch over tassel head (diagram B).

ABOVE: Sewing Chatelaine.
Basket, pins, threads: From Lois with Love

Folk Art

Folk art is a decorative application of paint on wood, glass, paper, ceramic or tin surfaces. Traditionally it was done by peasants who would paint furniture or household articles to make their homes more attractive. The projects we have featured are suitable for beginners, and require practice rather than artistic skill.

BASIC EQUIPMENT
Paint palette (a plate will do)
Acrylic paints (we used Jo Sonja's acrylics)
Stylus (a darning needle in a cork or an empty ball-point pen will do)
Brushes (four brushes were used for the strokes on our folk art projects: size 12 Roymac imitation sable large flat brush; size 3 Drawell golden nylon round brush; size 4 Raphael 8220 liner brush; size 12 Raphael 8230 small flat shader brush)
Very fine sandpaper
Paper towel
Adhesive tape
Cotton buds
Chalk paper (for substitute, rub blackboard chalk over writing paper and brush off excess chalk before using)
Sealer (we used Jo Sonja's sealer)
Varnish (we used Jo Sonja's varnish)
Tracing paper
Pencil

TECHNIQUES
Painting. Squeeze a small amount of paint onto palette. Wet the round brush with water. Roll brush onto paper towel to remove excess water. Gently pat brush into paint until fibres are covered to just below ferrule (about ¾ covered).
Comma stroke. Hold the round brush at a 45 degree angle, as you would hold a pen. Steady your hand by placing your little finger on the painting surface. Touch the brush to painting surface then pull towards you, gently lifting the brush until it is held upright and only the tip is touching the surface. Slowly lift brush off surface. Practice, then try painting commas in different sizes and directions.

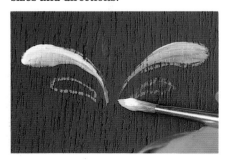

Filling in a shape. Always paint with careful strokes, following the shape to be filled.

Linework. Roll liner brush into a small amount of paint which has been thinned with water to consistency of ink. Wipe excess onto paper towel. Using brush upright (at a 90 degree angle), try lightly painting lines and circles. Practice writing and drawing with this brush.

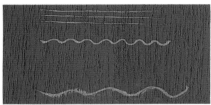

Dots. Dip stylus into undiluted fresh paint and dot onto paper to make tiny dots. Use wooden end of a brush in same way, to make large dots.

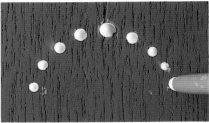

For dots of the same size, dip stylus or brush end into paint for each dot. For dots of descending size, continue dotting without dipping brush into paint.

Box with Roses

15cm-diameter round balsa box with lid
Acrylic paints, in carbon black, burgundy, rich gold, pine green and white
Size 12 Roymac imitation sable large flat brush
Size 4 Raphael 8220 liner brush
Size 3 Drawell golden nylon round brush
Size 12 Raphael 8230 small flat shader brush
Sealer
Varnish
Chalk paper

Pencil and tracing paper
Very fine sandpaper
Paper towel
Adhesive tape
Stylus

Read Basic Equipment and Technique notes on page 8.

 Cut tracing paper same size as box lid. Draw design at left onto paper, sizing it to fit lid. Sand box joints smooth.

Using the large flat brush, paint lid inside and out with a mixture of 1 part burgundy to 1 part sealer. Paint box inside and out with a mixture of 1 part black to 1 part sealer. When dry, lightly sand all outside painted surfaces.

Tape design on lid, leaving enough room to slip chalk paper, chalk side down, between paper and lid of box. Trace inner circle with a stylus, applying enough pressure to leave a chalk tracing on the box lid.

Remove design and paint inner circle black. Allow paint to dry. (A hair dryer can be used to speed drying time.)

Place design on lid as before and trace complete design.

Paint lines using the liner brush and thinned gold paint.

Load round brush with green paint, picking up a little gold on one side. Use this to paint leaves. Fill in leaf shapes, rinse brush well.

Load round brush with burgundy and fill in rose shape. Add small amount of black to burgundy, shade centre and underneath rose; rinse the brush well.

Place commas of gold over roses using round brush.

Using stylus, place small white dots in rose centre.

Dip handle end of brush in white paint and place dots in centre of intersecting lines.

Using small flat brush and thinned gold paint, add border around the outer circle, over burgundy, around edge of lid. Dot around this circle with gold using handle end of small flat brush.

Brush thinned gold over black on box bottom. Rub off with wet paper towel to give an antique finish.

Erase all chalk marks when paint is dry. Apply 2 coats of varnish.

BELOW: Box with Roses.

Made by Anne Colligan

Made by Anne Colligan

Daisy Box

12.5cm-diameter round balsa box
   with lid
Acrylic paints, in teal green, sapphire,
   aqua and white
Size 12 Roymac imitation sable large
   flat brush
Size 4 Raphael 8220 liner brush
Sealer
Varnish
Chalk paper
Pencil and tracing paper
Fine sandpaper
Adhesive tape
Stylus

Read Basic Equipment and Technique
notes on page 8.

Cut tracing paper to fit box lid. Draw
design outline, shown at right, onto
paper, sizing it to fit box lid. Sand box
joints smooth.

Prepare a paint mixture of 1 part
teal green paint to 1 part sealer. Use
large flat brush to paint mixture on lid.

Paint bottom of box with a mixture
of 1 part sapphire to 1 part sealer.
When dry, lightly sand box again.

Tape design on lid, leaving enough
room to slip chalk paper, chalk side
down, between paper and lid of box.

Trace design with a stylus, applying
enough pressure to leave chalk tracing

on the box lid.

Remove papers and tape, paint intersecting lines using liner brush with
thinned aqua paint. Paint circle around
lines with a wavy line in aqua.

Using the handle end of the brush,
make dots of white for flower centres at
points where lines intersect. Add 4 dots
in sapphire around white centre dots.

Work even-sized dots in white over
outer circle, next to top edge of box lid.

Lightly dip the large flat brush into
small amounts of teal green and aqua
and streak these colours over the sapphire on sides and bottom of box base.

Erase all chalk marks when paint is
dry. Apply 2 coats of varnish.

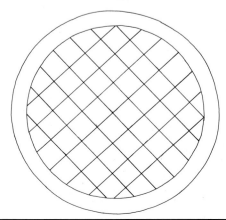

Small Pink Terracotta Pot

Small terracotta pot
Acrylic paints, in pale pink, crimson,
   pine green, black and white
Size 12 Roymac imitation sable large
   flat brush
Size 3 Drawell golden nylon round
   brush
White chalk pencil
Cotton buds
Ruler or tape measure
Stylus

Read Basic Equipment and Technique
notes on page 8.

Using the large flat brush, paint en-
tire pot with pale pink.

Using chalk pencil, mark dots, about
3cm apart, around upper edge of pot.
Refer to picture at right when painting
this design.

Dip cotton bud into crimson paint on
one side of the tip and white on the
other side of same tip.

Press the paint loaded tip firmly
onto chalk mark; twist cotton bud. This
will make a swirl of crimson and white
like a tiny rose.

Using stylus, paint a small black
centre in each tiny rose and place 3 tiny
white dots on the black to highlight the
rose centre.

Using green, paint 3 small comma
strokes on each side of the rose, using
round brush.

Dip stylus or brush end into white
paint and mark dots in decreasing sizes
between roses.

Erase all chalk marks when paint is
thoroughly dry.

Terracotta Pot with Hearts

Small terracotta pot
Acrylic paints, in moss green, pine
   green, crimson, yellow and white
Size 12 Roymac imitation sable large
   flat brush
Size 3 Drawell golden nylon round
   brush
Chalk paper
Tracing paper and pencil
Adhesive tape
Stylus

Read Basic Equipment and Technique
notes on page 8.

Load large flat brush with moss
green paint. Placing one side of brush
under pot rim, pull brush around pot to
make a border. Allow paint to dry.

Trace design on page 11 onto tracing
paper. Tape design to pot and slip chalk
paper under design, chalk side next to
pot. Trace design with a stylus; remove
design and chalk paper.

Paint hearts in crimson using round brush. Rinse brush well.

Use round brush to paint pine green comma shapes and lines.

Using brush handle, dab five dots to make small white daisies in centre of hearts and at each side of design. Place one white dot between hearts. Add yellow daisy centres.

Erase all chalk marks when paint is thoroughly dry.

Strawberry Butter Spreader

Wooden butter spreader
Acrylic paints, in crimson, pine green, yellow and white
Size 3 Drawell golden nylon round brush
Varnish
Chalk paper
Very fine sandpaper
Tracing paper and pencil
Stylus

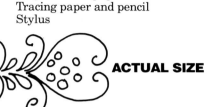

ACTUAL SIZE

Read Basic Equipment and Technique notes on page 8.

Lightly sand spreader. Trace design on page 12 and cut tracing paper to fit spreader. Place design on one side of butter spreader with chalk paper under design, chalk side next to spreader. Holding firmly in place, trace design with stylus; remove papers. (This design may also be drawn freehand.)

Paint strawberry with round brush, using crimson.

Using stylus, make 3 tiny white dot daisies with yellow centres, on the strawberry as pictured.

Paint green comma strokes for leaves, using round brush. Add dainty lines in green to handle of spreader to

LEFT: Daisy Box. BELOW: Small Pink Terracotta Pot, Terracotta Pot with Hearts, Floral Butter Spreader, Strawberry Butter Spreader.

Below: Picture, clock: Flossoms

Made by Anne Colligan

create leaves, using round brush.

Using the stylus, make a white dot daisy and dot clusters at other end of butter spreader.

Dot daisy centre yellow. Make tiny red dots between daisy petals.

Erase all chalk marks when paint is thoroughly dry. Apply a coat of varnish.

ACTUAL SIZE

ACTUAL SIZE

Floral Butter Spreader

Wooden butter spreader
Acrylic paints, in pink, pine green, yellow oxide, sapphire blue and white
Size 3 Drawell golden nylon round brush
Varnish
Chalk paper
Very fine sandpaper
Tracing paper and pencil
Stylus

Read Basic Equipment and Technique notes on page 8.

Lightly sand butter spreader. Trace design above and cut paper to fit spreader. Place design on one side of butter spreader with chalk paper under design, chalk side next to spreader. Holding firmly in place, trace design with a stylus; remove papers. (This design may also be drawn freehand.)

Load the round brush with pink paint, lightly dip into white, and paint long comma strokes along handle of butter spreader.

Rinse brush well, load with pine green and paint small leaves.

Dip brush handle into sapphire blue and dot on the daisy petals.

When blue dots are dry, dip handle into yellow and dot the centres.

Dot around daisy centres with stylus dipped in white and make clusters of 3 dots, in white, along the handle of the spreader.

Erase all chalk marks when paint is thoroughly dry. Apply a coat of varnish.

Handmade Book

5-8 sheets A4 writing or drawing paper, or size desired
Heavy paper (for book cover; can be decorated with watercolour paints or inks, see Bookmark, page 20; or decorated with a paste-paper technique, see Paste-paper, page 121)
Six stranded embroidery thread or linen thread
Awl or large darning needle
Blunt knife
Pegs or bulldog clips

Cut A4 paper into quarters (or desired page size).

Cut 2 pieces of heavy paper same size as pages, for front and back covers.

Mark evenly spaced positions for holes along left edge of front cover. There must be an odd number of holes; marks can be in line with each other or in a zigzag pattern along book edge.

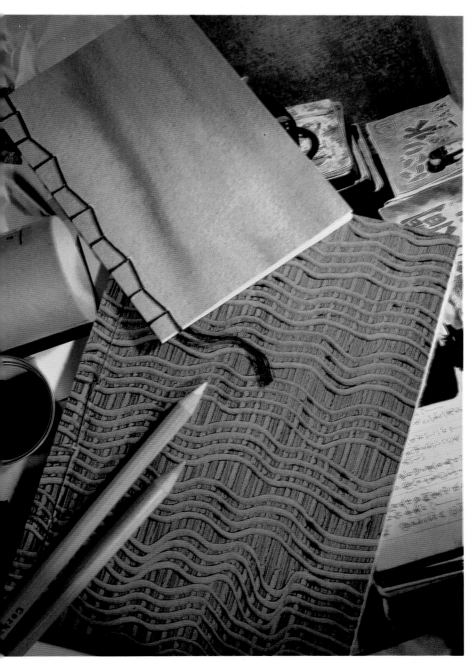

LEFT and ABOVE: Handmade Book.

Teddy

Our embroidered teddy has arms and legs attached with joints. If joints are unavailable, use strong twine and a long needle to secure arms and legs in place. Take a stitch through top of one arm, through body from one side to the other, then through other arm. Repeat until secure. Attach legs in the same way.

40cm x 120cm-wide wool fabric
Polyester fibre filling
4 x 35mm joints (from specialist craft stores)
Black linen twine (for nose)
1 pair glass bear eyes (from specialist craft stores) or black stranded embroidery thread
Tapestry wool in selection of pastel colours
Size 20 tapestry needle
Thread
Water-soluble pen

Height: 50cm approximately
Make pattern from graph. See page 126 for enlarging instructions. Cut fabric using pattern. Pattern has 5mm seam allowances. Double stitch all seams for extra strength. Stitch around all corners to reinforce. Clip all curved seams and corners, after stitching.

Head. Stitch darts at neck edge on each Side Head piece. Pin and stitch Side Head pieces right sides together, along centre front seam from nose to neck. Starting at nose, and spacing pins 5mm apart, pin Centre Head piece between Side Head pieces, matching notches and easing to fit. Stitch. Turn right side out.

Ears. Place two Ear pieces right sides together for each ear and stitch, leaving lower edges open. Turn right side out, turn in raw edges along lower edge and handstitch together.

Body. Place Body Front pieces right sides together and stitch centre front seam. With Body Back pieces right sides together, stitch centre back seam, leaving open the neck edge and a space for stuffing. Place Body Front and Body Back right sides together; match notches and stitch side seams. Turn right side out.

Legs. Using two pieces for each Leg and placing right sides facing, pin Leg pieces together. Stitch around Legs, leaving opening for stuffing and leave notched edge open. Pin Foot Pads into legs, right sides together and matching notches. Stitch, turn right side out.

Arms. Placing right sides together, stitch around Inside and Outside Arms, leaving openings for stuffing. Turn right side out.

Using a blunt knife, so paper is not cut, score a line on front cover from top to bottom edge next to hole markings. Score back cover in same position. These will form cover fold lines.

Place pages and covers together, hold in place with pegs or bulldog clips.

Punch holes through book at positions marked, using an awl or large darning needle.

To stitch book together. Cut thread 4 times book length plus about 25cm. Starting at top back of book, thread needle through first hole.

Take thread over top edge of book and back through first hole (from back of book). Bring thread around side edge (from front of book) and through the first hole again.

Take thread down and through second hole, around side edge and through the second hole again. Take thread down to third hole and continue until last hole is threaded. Take thread around bottom edge of book (from back of book) and through last hole again (from front of book), return to top through holes using running stitch to fill any spaces.

Tie ends of thread together, trim.

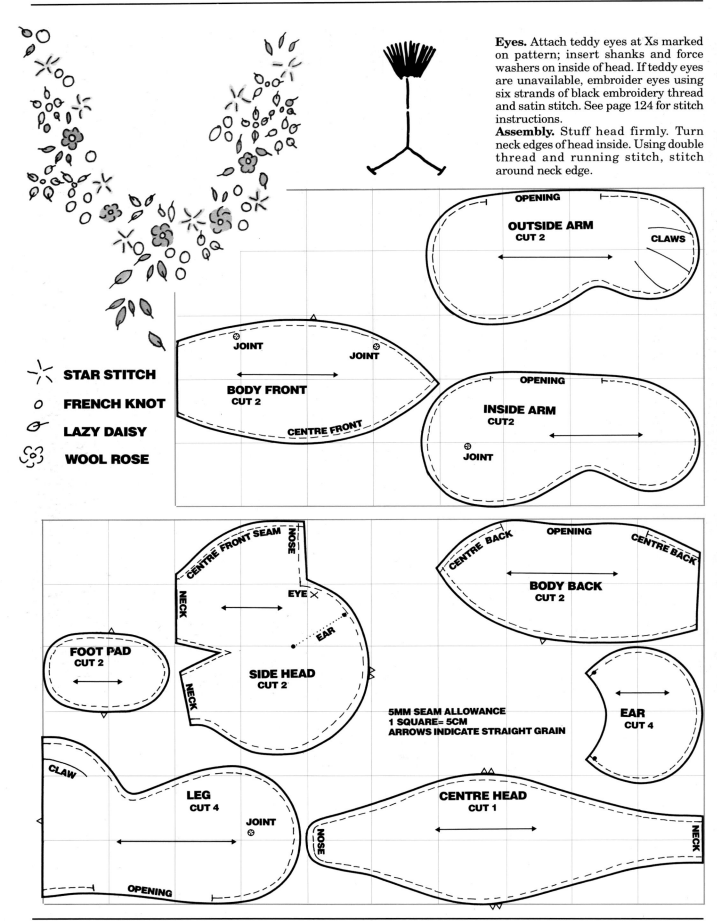

Eyes. Attach teddy eyes at Xs marked on pattern; insert shanks and force washers on inside of head. If teddy eyes are unavailable, embroider eyes using six strands of black embroidery thread and satin stitch. See page 124 for stitch instructions.

Assembly. Stuff head firmly. Turn neck edges of head inside. Using double thread and running stitch, stitch around neck edge.

STAR STITCH

FRENCH KNOT

LAZY DAISY

WOOL ROSE

OUTSIDE ARM
CUT 2

CLAWS

OPENING

BODY FRONT
CUT 2

CENTRE FRONT

JOINT

JOINT

INSIDE ARM
CUT 2

OPENING

JOINT

FOOT PAD
CUT 2

CENTRE FRONT SEAM

NOSE

NECK

EYE

EAR

NECK

SIDE HEAD
CUT 2

CENTRE BACK

OPENING

CENTRE BACK

BODY BACK
CUT 2

EAR
CUT 4

5MM SEAM ALLOWANCE
1 SQUARE = 5CM
ARROWS INDICATE STRAIGHT GRAIN

CLAW

LEG
CUT 4

JOINT

OPENING

NOSE

CENTRE HEAD
CUT 1

NECK

Made by From Lois with Love (02) 969 6847 (classes available)

Insert joints into limbs at positions marked on pattern, then stuff limbs and body until firm. Except for neck edges, handstitch openings closed using double thread. Handstitch neck to body securely. Handstitch ears to head at positions marked on pattern, easing ears to fit.

Nose and mouth. Using linen twine, embroider a nose in satin stitch and work a mouth using straight stitches. See diagram at top left.

Embroidery. Using tapestry wool and needle, work necklace in stem stitch. Work bow in stem stitch at the centre front of body.

Transfer actual size flower garland design, at top left, onto bear's chest using water-soluble pen. Using tapestry needle and wool in colours of your choice work design in stitches marked on diagram. Embroider a wool rose with lazy daisy stitches for leaves on sole of each foot.

ABOVE: Teddy.

Pram: Keyhole Furniture

Hearts-and-Flowers Set

TISSUE COVER

19cm x 15cm 14-count Aida fabric
2 x 15cm x 5cm pieces cotton fabric
(for lining)
DMC six stranded embroidery thread
(see key for colours, one skein each
colour)
Tapestry needle
Thread

Size: 12.5cm x 8.5cm.
1cm seam allowance included.

Embroider design from graph below using two strands of thread. Work in cross-stitch in colours indicated on key. Each symbol represents one cross-stitch embroidered over one fabric square. See page 124 for embroidery stitch instructions.

Position design across both 15cm ends of Aida fabric. Begin by stitching pale pink line 18mm from raw edge and 10mm from sides. When design at one end is complete, repeat at other end, positioning embroidery in same way.

Matching 15cm edges, position one lining piece over embroidered fabric, right sides together. Stitch 15cm edges together. Repeat with second lining piece at opposite end. Neaten remaining 15cm edges of lining.

Turn lining to wrong side of embroidered fabric and press. Fold fabric in half across width to find centre, mark with a pin. Open out fabric and fold both 15cm edges in, to meet at centre mark, right sides together. Stitch raw edges along each side, neaten seams. Turn right side out.

Press, embroidered side down, on a padded surface.

HAND TOWEL

4.5cm-wide 14-count Aida band, 3cm
longer than towel width
DMC six stranded embroidery thread
(see key for colours, one skein
each colour)
Tapestry needle
Thread

Embroider design from graph below using two strands of thread. Work in cross-stitch, in colours indicated on key. Each symbol represents one cross-stitch embroidered over one fabric square. See page 124 for embroidery stitch instructions.

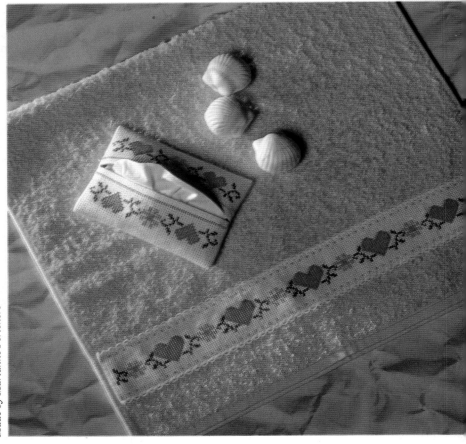

Made by Marianne Porteners

Position heart motif in centre of Aida band. When motif, including border, is complete, there will be one row unworked at top and bottom of band.

Repeat design as many times as required along length of band. Our example shows a total of 5 hearts and 6 flower motifs. Press completed band from wrong side on a padded surface. Turn raw ends of embroidered work under, position band approximately 5cm from lower edge of towel and stitch in place by hand or machine.

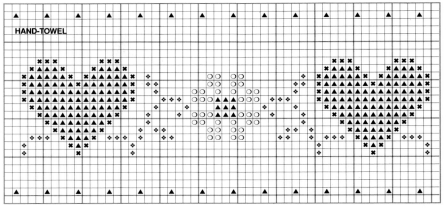

HAND-TOWEL

	DMC No.
❖ Green	503
○ Pale pink	3326
▲ Pink	899
✖ Deep pink	335

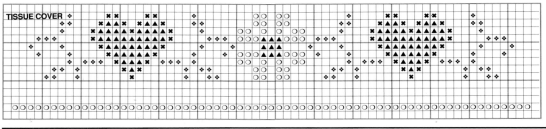

TISSUE COVER

Stocking and Ring Bag

1.3m x 115cm-wide organza fabric
2m x 1.5cm-wide ribbon
40cm x 3.5cm-wide ribbon
50cm cord
Thread

STOCKING BAG
Cut 2 organza pieces 43cm x 37cm for Back. Cut 3 organza pieces 46cm x 37cm for Pockets. 1cm seam included.

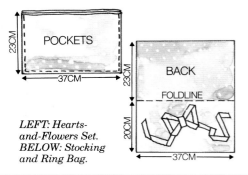

LEFT: Hearts-and-Flowers Set. BELOW: Stocking and Ring Bag.

Bow applique. Fold 1.5cm-wide ribbon into a bow, using separate lengths of ribbon to form bow loops and ties. Pin and tack bow across 37cm end of one Back piece. Handstitch in place.

Fold Back pieces across 37cm-width, 23cm from bottom edge; press.

Fold Pocket pieces in half, right sides together, to give 3 doubled pieces 37cm x 23cm; press. Tack all pocket pieces together along two narrow edges and long raw edge.

Place the Pocket pieces between the 2 Back sections, right sides together, at opposite end to bow applique. Stitch around 3 sides leaving applique end open, turn right side out and press.

Press 3.5cm-wide ribbon in half lengthways. Place over open end of bag and fold ribbon ends under to fit bag. Pin and stitch ribbon in place.

RING BAG
Cut 35cm x 14cm organza piece for bag and 25cm x 14cm piece for lining.

Fold bag piece in half, across width, wrong sides together. Foldline will be at bottom of bag. Stitch ribbon bow onto one half of bag piece following directions for bow applique on stocking bag.

Fold bag piece in half, this time with right sides together. Fold lining piece in the same way.

Stitch side seams of both bag and lining using 1cm seam allowance and leaving a 1cm opening in one side seam, 25mm from top edge, for cord. Turn bag only right side out.

Press 5mm hem on top edge of both bag and lining. Insert lining into bag.

Pin together at top so that lining hem is about 3mm down from top edge of bag, on the inside of bag. Stitch around top edge, securing lining to bag. Make casing by stitching 2 more rows through both layers, 15mm from top and 25mm from top. Insert cord through casing, knot cord ends.

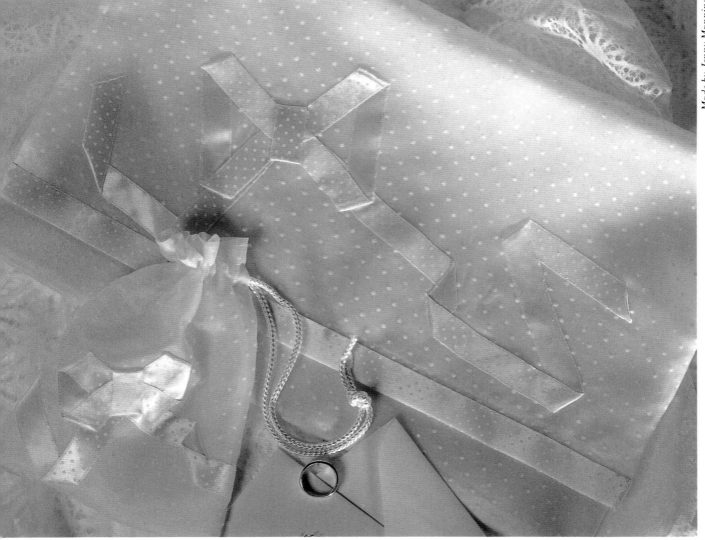

Made by Jenny Manning

Calico doll

40cm x 115cm-wide calico fabric
Fabric paint, in white, brown, black
    and red
Glaze (optional, we used Matisse Gel
    MM4, available from art supply
    stores)
Polyester fibre filling
Thread
Paint brush
2B pencil

Enlarge pattern following instructions
on page 126.

Note. Cut Nose pieces actual size. Cut
out pattern pieces in calico and mark
dots with pencil. 5mm seam allowance
is included.

Place 2 Leg pieces right sides
together, stitch around Leg pieces,
leaving straight (top) edge open. Clip
curves; turn right side out. Repeat for
other leg.

Place 2 Arm pieces right sides
together, stitch around Arm pieces,
leaving straight edge open. Clip curves;
turn right side out. Repeat for other
arm.

Fill legs and arms with polyester
fibre to dotted lines, pack fibre tightly,
using a wooden spoon handle to push it
down.

With seams of legs and arms at
centre front (so toes and hands face
front) machine stitch along dotted lines
on legs and arms, using zipper foot.

Press seam allowance along bottom
edge of Back piece to wrong side. Stitch
legs to bottom edge of Back between
dots, placing raw edges together.

Stitch arms to Back between side
dots, placing raw edges together.

Place Nose pieces right sides
together, stitch from one small dot,
through large dot, to other small dot.
Turn right side out. Pin nose on Left
Front piece, matching small dots and
placing raw edges together. Tack nose
in place.

Stitch Left Front and Right Front
pieces together between large dots.
Press seam allowance to wrong side
along stitching line and along bottom
edge of Front pieces. Place Back and
Front right sides together, arms and
legs inside body, and pin.

Stitch around curved edge of body,
leaving bottom edge open. Turn right
side out.

Pin Front and Back together at
lower edge of body, machine stitch
(stitching line forms joint between legs
and body, allowing legs to move).

LEFT: Calico Doll.

Chair: Balmain Linen and Lace. Mat: Mosmania.
Cupboard: Copeland and de Soos

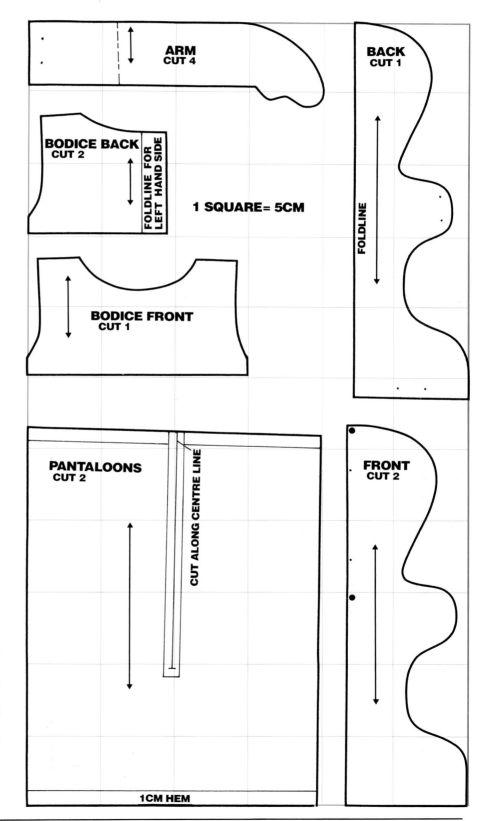

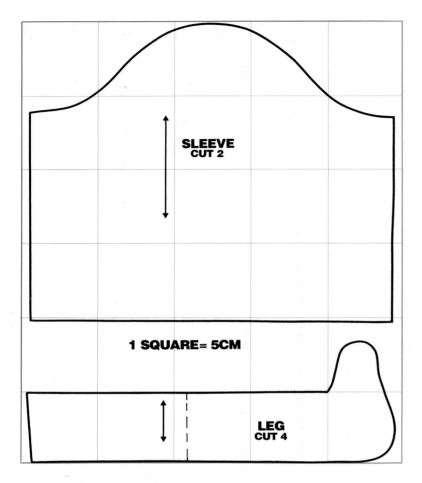

SLEEVE
CUT 2

1 SQUARE= 5CM

LEG
CUT 4

Fill body with polyester fibre through front opening, pack filling tightly. Handstitch opening closed.

To paint. Outline hairline, shoes, eyes and mouth using 2B pencil and using picture as a guide.

Mix a little brown with white paint to give a skin tone. Paint face, neck, hands and legs. A slightly blotchy, imperfect finish is more effective than a perfect one. Paint cheeks, using slightly darker skin colour made by adding more brown paint.

When paint is dry, paint hair, eyes and shoes using black. Paint mouth, using a mixture of brown and red.

Leave to dry overnight then press lightly to heat-fix paint. Paint doll with glaze, if desired.

DRESS AND PANTALOONS

50cm x 115cm-wide cotton fabric
(for Dress)
10cm x 115cm-wide cotton fabric
(for Bodice Frill)
30cm x 115cm-wide cotton fabric
(for Pantaloons)
20cm x 3cm bias strip cotton fabric
(for Neck Binding)
Motif (optional)
Small button
Thread

Enlarge pattern following instructions on page 126. Cut pattern pieces in fabrics listed above. In addition, cut Skirt piece 64cm x 27cm. 5mm seam allowance is included.

Dress. Fold 115cm x 10cm Bodice Frill piece in half lengthways, right sides together. Stitch across ends, turn right side out; press. Stitch 2 gathering rows along raw edge.

Stitch Front Bodice to Back Bodice pieces at shoulders. Press a 5mm hem along centre back of right Back Bodice piece. Press along fold line at centre back of left Back Bodice piece. Overlap left over right by 1cm, tack together at lower edge.

Pin Frill to one armhole, across lower edge of Front Bodice, then up around remaining armhole; adjust gathers to fit.

Stitch 2 gathering rows around top of Sleeve. Stitch 1cm hem on Sleeve ends. Pin Sleeves into armhole over Frill, right sides together. Adjust gathers to fit; stitch.

Fold Skirt piece in half across width, right sides together. Pin and stitch along narrow edges of Skirt, press.

Stitch 2.5cm hem on Skirt. Fold and stitch a 1cm-wide tuck around Skirt,

6cm up from hem edge.

Stitch 2 gathering rows along upper edge of Skirt. Pin Skirt to Front and Back Bodice pieces, right sides together. Adjust gathers to fit; stitch and neaten seam.

Stitch bias binding to neckline, folding under ends of bias flush with back bodice opening. See page 125 for bias instructions.

Put dress on doll. Overlap bias ends at back neck, sew button onto bias, stitching through both ends of bias. Handstitch a row of gathering around Sleeve ends. Pull up gathers, sew Sleeve ends to doll's wrists.

Stitch motif to Front Bodice, if desired.

Pantaloons. Stitch 1cm hem at waist and ankles of Pantaloon pieces. Place Pantaloon pieces right sides together, pin and stitch side seams; turn right side out. Handstitch a row of gathering around waist. Fit Pantaloons to doll, stitch in place at waist.

Bookmark

Heavy paper (writing paper, art, or water-colour paper)
Watercolour paints or inks (to decorate paper)
Paint brush
Pencil
Scalpel or craft knife

Mark a 22cm x 4.5cm rectangle on paper and paint rectangle as desired, using paints or inks.

Cut out rectangle. Fold in half lengthways.

Starting 25mm from top edge, mark folded edge of paper with pencil at 7mm intervals, leave 7mm border at bottom edge (see diagram at right). All measurements must be accurate.

Starting 10mm from top edge, mark 2 rows of dots at 15mm intervals, 12mm and 17mm from folded edge. Draw dotted lines from 12mm and 17mm marks out to 7mm marks along fold, as shown in diagram.

Cut out two V-shaped sections at top of bookmark using knife. Cut through fold along each dotted line.

Open out bookmark. Starting below the 2 cut-out V-shapes, fold every second V-shaped section up. Beginning from the top again, weave the points of each section under and over each other (refer to picture).

ABOVE RIGHT: Bow Hat.
RIGHT: Bookmark.

Above right: Rug, cushion: Sandy de Beyer

Bow Hat

Straw hat
6 strips 20cm x 115cm-wide
    co-ordinating cotton fabrics
Thread
Large needle

Cut 5 strips of fabric, 70cm x 16cm, for bows. 1cm seam allowance included.

Fold in half lengthways, right sides together. Stitch along 70cm raw edge, turn right side out, press. Tie each length into a bow. Cut ends diagonally, turn raw edges in and slip-stitch.

Cut remaining fabric into a 60cm x 7cm strip, or length to fit around hat crown. Fold in half lengthways, right sides together. Stitch along 60cm raw edge of band. Turn right side out; press. Pin band ends together around hat crown. Pin bows in position around band. Remove band from hat, hand-stitch bows in place.

Return band to crown of hat, stitch band ends together. Tack band securely to hat using double thread.

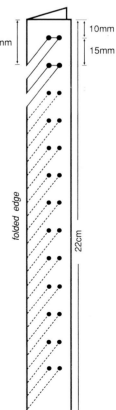

25mm

10mm

15mm

folded edge

22cm

Made by Jenny Manning

FRONT AND BACK (DOTTED LINE)

1 SQUARE= 5CM

BOW

TIE

Hair-Ribbon Holder

20cm x 90cm-wide fabric
2 x 10cm x 90cm-wide contrasting
　fabrics (for Bow and Tie)
30cm square wadding
14cm narrow ribbon
Thick cardboard (we used 10-sheet
　pasteboard)
Scalpel or craft knife
Paper clips or pegs
2-3 silk flowers (optional)
Craft glue
Thread

Enlarge pattern at left following instructions on page 126. Using pattern, cut cardboard for Front, Bow and Tie.

Cut Back, making it 2mm smaller all around than Front (indicated on pattern by dotted line).

Cut fabric for each piece including Back, allowing an extra 1.5cm all around each pattern piece. Use contrasting fabric for Bow and Tie.

Glue wadding to each cardboard piece except Back. Trim wadding to fit.

Glue fabric over each piece to cover wadding. Glue fabric to Back piece. Clip curves and corners and glue excess fabric to back. Hold fabric in place with paper clips or pegs until glue sets.

Cut fabric for back of Bow and Tie; make these pieces slightly smaller than pattern. Glue in place. Glue Tie to centre top of Front and glue Bow on top of Tie.

Cut a strip of fabric 15cm x 3.5cm and press 15cm-long raw edges to fabric centre. Place strip firmly around centre of Bow and stitch securely.

Glue ends of ribbon to Front at top, to make a loop for hanging.

Glue flowers in place, hold with a paper clip or peg until dry. Glue Back in place, using paper clips or pegs until glue dries.

Scrunchy Set

SCRUNCHIES
For each scrunchy:
20cm x 115cm-wide fabric
25cm elastic
Thread

Cut 110cm x 14cm fabric strip.

Press 5mm hem at each narrow end of fabric. Fold in half lengthways, right sides together. Pin and stitch along length 1cm from raw edges. Turn right side out and press.

Insert elastic through fabric tube and stitch elastic ends together firmly. Handstitch fabric ends together.

Note. Scrunchies can be made in various widths as desired.

HOLDER
Wooden paper towel holder
Undercoat paint
Enamel paint
Paintbrush
Fine sandpaper
Mineral turpentine (for cleaning brush)

Sand surface of towel holder lightly, apply undercoat. Once dry, apply two coats of enamel paint, allowing each coat to dry and sanding lightly between each coat.

Made by Jenny Manning

LEFT: Hair-Ribbon Holder.
RIGHT: Scrunchy Set.

Made by Marianne Porteners

Australian Floral Emblems

Embroider Australian floral emblems on lavender sachets or frame them for an attractive hanging.

FRAGRANT SACHETS

For each sachet:

30cm x 10cm 14-count Aida fabric
DMC six stranded embroidery thread (see key for colours, one skein each colour)
Six stranded embroidery thread in grey (DMC No.318) (for lettering)
Narrow ribbon
Tapestry needle
Thread
Dried lavender
Fine white crochet yarn (optional)
1.25mm crochet hook (optional)

Size: 14cm x 9cm approximately.

		DMC No.
❖	Green	3347
▲	Red	304
✳	Dark red	814
■	Black	310
✖	Dark Green	904
I	Black	310
	(backstitch around flower centres)	
—	Dark Red	814
	(backstitch around flower)	
▬	Dark green (backstitch)	904

Fold fabric in half across width and crease. Open fabric out. Count five rows up from crease to start embroidery (this will be sachet front). See page 124 for embroidery stitch instructions.

Begin by working the name of emblem in backstitch, using two strands grey (No.318) thread. Work from graphs below and overpage. Centre graph design on sachet front. Each symbol represents one cross-stitch embroidered over one fabric square using two strands of thread in colours indicated on key.

Work outlines in backstitch using one strand of thread.

To complete sachet, stitch narrow hems on both 10cm edges of fabric. Fold fabric on crease line, right sides together, and stitch along side seams using 5mm seams. Neaten seams, turn sachet right side out and gently push out corners.

Crochet edging (optional). Using crochet yarn, embroider a row of blanket stitch, two fabric squares deep and two apart, along sachet edge to form base loops for crochet.

LEFT: Australian Floral Emblems.

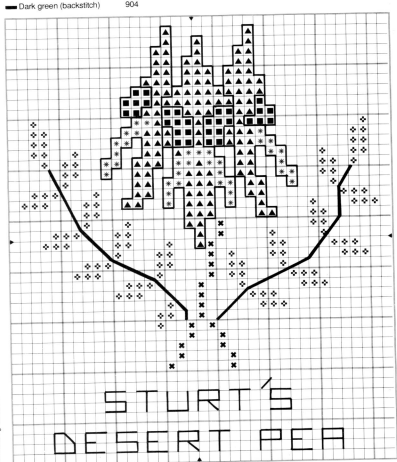

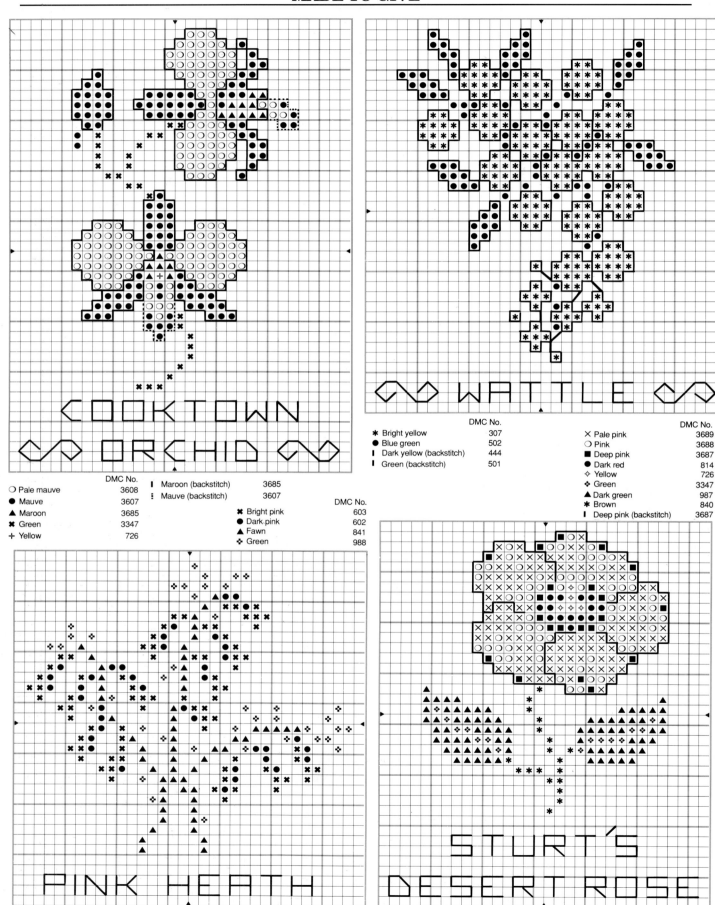

COOKTOWN ORCHID

	DMC No.		DMC No.
○ Pale mauve	3608	I Maroon (backstitch)	3685
● Mauve	3607	¦ Mauve (backstitch)	3607
▲ Maroon	3685		
✖ Green	3347		DMC No.
+ Yellow	726	✖ Bright pink	603
		● Dark pink	602
		▲ Fawn	841
		❖ Green	988

WATTLE

	DMC No.		DMC No.
✱ Bright yellow	307	✕ Pale pink	3689
● Blue green	502	○ Pink	3688
I Dark yellow (backstitch)	444	■ Deep pink	3687
I Green (backstitch)	501	● Dark red	814
		❖ Yellow	726
		❖ Green	3347
		▲ Dark green	987
		✱ Brown	840
		I Deep pink (backstitch)	3687

PINK HEATH

STURT'S DESERT ROSE

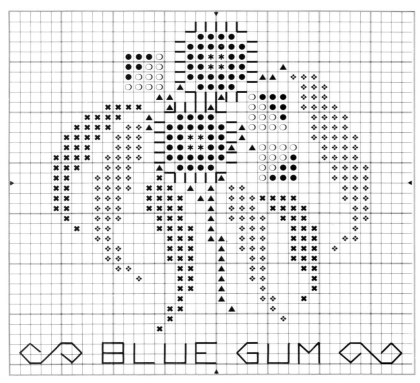

First row: 2 double crochet (dc) in each base loop, slip-stitch (sl st) to first dc.

Second row: *1dc in next dc, 2 treble (tr) in next dc, 1dc in next dc, 1sl st in next dc, repeat from * to end, sl st to first st, fasten off.

Gently press finished sachet from wrong side on a padded surface. Fill with lavender and tie with ribbon, making a bow.

FRAMED EMBROIDERIES

Work as for sachets, using 15cm squares of 14-count Aida fabric, and frame as individual miniatures. Alternatively, work emblems on a 55cm x 35cm piece of 14-count Aida fabric. Position emblems in two rows of four, spacing equally. Frame as desired.

		DMC No.
❖	Light green	502
✖	Dark green	501
●	Pale yellow	677
✳	Olive	581
○	Grey	647
▲	Brown	839
I	Pale yellow (backstitch)	677

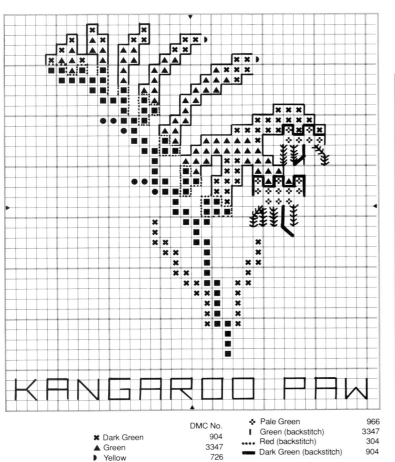

		DMC No.
✖	Dark Green	904
▲	Green	3347
▸	Yellow	726
■	Red	304
●	Dark Red	814
❖	Pale Green	966
I	Green (backstitch)	3347
....	Red (backstitch)	304
▬	Dark Green (backstitch)	904
⫷⫷⫷	Yellow (backstitch)	726

		DMC No.			
▼	Red	304	✱	Deep fawn	840
✖	Dark Green	3345	■	Dark brown	839
❖	Green	3347	I	Burgundy (backstitch around flower)	814
●	Dark red	815			
▸	Pale pink	818	I	Dark Green (backstitch around leaves)	3345

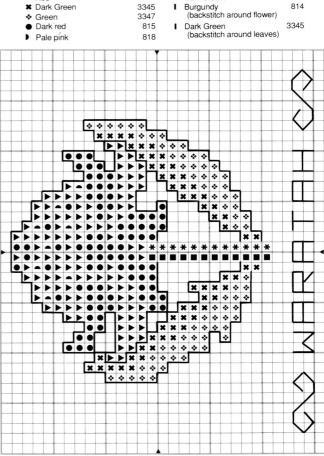

Guest Towel

70cm x 135cm bath towel
30cm x 90cm-wide fine lawn fabric
1.5m x 3cm-wide double-sided taffeta
    or satin ribbon
Thread

Cut 2 strips of lawn, 90cm x 20cm and 90cm x 10cm.

Fold the 20cm strip lengthways, wrong sides facing, raw edges together. Run a gathering thread along the long raw edges and gather until same width as towel. Pin and stitch gathered edge onto one end of towel.

Turn in 1cm along both long raw edges of the remaining fabric piece and press. Press narrow edges under to fit width of towel, trim excess. Stitch fabric flat onto end of towel to cover raw edge of frill.

Cut ribbon 2cm longer than towel width. Fold 1cm under at each end and press. Stitch ribbon onto towel, positioning it on the top edge of the 10cm-wide fabric piece.

Shape remaining ribbon into a bow. Pin bow flat onto ribbon and handstitch in place. Fold under and stitch raw ends.

BELOW: Guest Towel.
RIGHT: Paste-Paper Covered Books.

Made by From Lois with Love (02) 969 6847 (classes available)

Made by Michael Lester

Paste-Paper Covered Books

EXERCISE BOOK
Exercise book
Paste-paper (see instructions on page 121; our paper was patterned with a comb)
Adhesive tape

Open out book. Cut paper 2cm larger all around than book.

Place book onto wrong side of paper, fold excess paper onto inside covers folding in corners. Tape in place.

AUTOGRAPH BOOK
Heavy writing or drawing paper
Heavy cardboard
Paste-paper (see instructions on page 121; our paper was patterned with a roller)
Glue stick
Strong thread (we used linen twine)
Scalpel or craft knife
Blunt knife
Awl or large darning needle

Cut 2 pieces cardboard, in desired size, for front and back cover. Cut pieces of heavy paper slightly smaller for pages.

Cut paste-paper 2cm larger all around than each cover piece. Apply glue to wrong side of paste-paper. Position cover in centre of paste-paper, trim diagonally across corners. Fold excess paper onto wrong side of cover, glue in place.

Cut 2 pieces of heavy paper same size as pages. Glue onto wrong side of each cover piece.

Using blunt knife, score along spine edge of each cover piece, about 10-15mm from edge (depending on book size); take care not to cut through the paper.

Place pages between front and back cover. Align edges along spine and pierce two holes between spine edge and scored line, positioning them equal distances from top and bottom edge of book.

Pass thread through holes, knot ends together (use more than one strand if desired).

CONCERTINA BOOK
Large sheet heavy writing or drawing paper
Heavy cardboard
Paste-paper (see instructions on page 121; our paper was patterned with a jar lid)
Glue stick
Scalpel or craft knife

Cut 2 cardboard pieces, 17cm x 8.5cm, for front and back covers. Cut 56cm x 16.5cm strip of heavy paper for pages.

Fold up 8cm on one end of heavy paper. Fold under 8cm on same end, continue folding every 8cm, alternating directions until a concertina shape is formed (making 8 separate pages).

Cut paste-paper 1cm larger all around than cover pieces. Apply glue to wrong side of paste-paper. Position a cover piece in centre of each paste-paper piece. Trim corners diagonally, fold excess paper onto wrong side of cover, glue in place.

Centre a page on inside front cover, glue in place. Repeat at other end with back cover.

Fold pages to close book.

Made by Julie Palmer

Calico Bunnies

Enlarge patterns following instructions on page 126.

70cm x 150cm-wide calico for each bunny

Six stranded embroidery thread in black and brown

Polyester fibre filling

Dressmaker's pencil

Thread

Height: 54cm approximately

Cut fabric using pattern. Mark notches, darts etc. with pencil. Pattern has 5mm seam allowances.

Head. Pin 2 Ear pieces, right sides facing. Stitch together leaving base open. Clip curves and neaten raw edges; turn right side out and press. Stitch small dots together to make tuck in Ear. Repeat for other Ear.

Sew darts in Side Head pieces, press dart towards back. Attach an Ear to each Side Head piece by tacking close to raw edge between dots. Ear tuck should face back.

Pin and stitch Side Head pieces to either side of Centre Head piece, right sides together, matching notches and stitching from straight edge to X. Pin and stitch centre front seam of Side Head pieces, right sides together, from large dot at neck edge to X. Centre front seam forms bunny's chin. Trim and clip seam, turn right side out.

Legs. Fold Leg in half along foldline, right sides together. Stitch around Leg, leaving top open and allowing an opening for stuffing. Turn right side out and press; position seam at centre front of

Leg. Repeat for other Leg.

Arms. Assemble Arms in same way, leaving top of Arms open as well as an opening for stuffing.

Body. Place right sides of Body Front pieces together. Pin and stitch centre front seam. Place Legs between dots on Body Front, and Arms below X. Arm and Leg seams should be at front so toes and hands face front.

Stitch dart in Body Back pieces. Place Body Back pieces right sides together. Pin and stitch centre back seam, leaving opening for stuffing as marked on pattern. Pin Body Front to Body Back, right sides together, Legs and Arms inside body. Pin and stitch together leaving neck open. Trim seam and clip curves.

Push head into body through neck

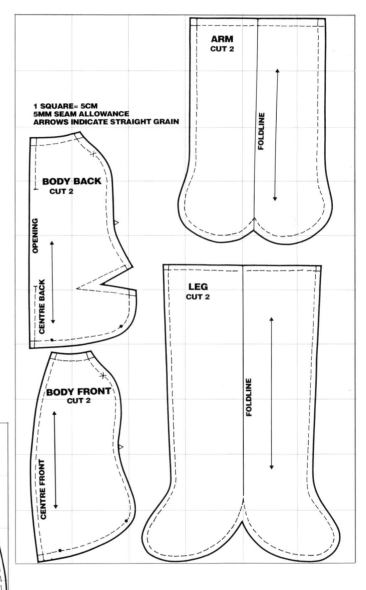

LEFT: Calico Bunnies.

Left: Chair: Keyhole Furniture

opening. Pin and stitch head to body around neck, right sides together. Centre front seam of head should match centre front seam of body. Turn right side out.

Insert stuffing through openings. Head should be stuffed quite firmly but leave body, arms and legs loosely stuffed and floppy. Slip-stitch all openings closed.

Embroidery. Mark eye positions with pencil. Using three strands black embroidery thread, make an end knot, insert needle in centre of one eye then take through to opposite eye. Tug to give a slight indentation and secure with a stitch.

Embroider eye in satin stitch, then outline in backstitch. See page 124 for embroidery stitch instructions. Take thread through to other side and complete second eye.

Using three strands of brown thread work a triangular shape for nose and three straight stitches for mouth.

DRESS FOR GIRL BUNNY
50cm x 115cm-wide cotton fabric
40cm lace
60cm narrow ribbon
1 small press stud
Thread

Cut fabric using pattern. Pattern has 5mm seam allowances.

Pin 2 Back Dress pieces right sides together. Stitch centre back seam from hem to X. Neaten raw edges and press centre back open. Topstitch around back opening.

With right sides of Sleeve and Back Dress together, match notches and pin and sew shoulder seams. Neaten edges and press seam towards Sleeve. Attach Sleeves to Front Dress in same way.

Stitch 2 rows of gathering around neck edge. Draw up gathers evenly to fit Neck Binding.

Turn in and hem raw ends of lace. Gather lace to fit between centre backs of Neck Binding. Tack right sides of lace and Neck Binding together along seam line. Match centre front squares and centre backs on Neck Binding with marks on neck edge of Front and Back Dress. Pin and stitch right side of Neck Binding to right side of dress at neck edge, with lace in between. Fold in binding ends at centre back. Fold in raw edge of Neck Binding; fold Neck Binding in half and slip-stitch in place. Handstitch small press stud to back neck opening.

Turn Sleeve hem up 1cm then another 1cm. Stitch in place and press.

With right sides together, pin and stitch Sleeve and side seams, matching notches and seams. Neaten raw edges, clip curves and press.

Turn dress hem up 1cm, then another 1cm. Stitch and press in place.

Make a ribbon bow and handstitch onto centre front of dress.

SHIRT FOR BOY BUNNY
30cm x 115cm-wide cotton fabric
1 small press stud
Thread

Cut fabric using pattern. Pattern has 5mm seam allowances.

With right sides together, join Shirt Back pieces by stitching centre back seam from hem to X. Neaten raw edges and press open. Topstitch around back neck opening.

With right sides together, match notches, pin and stitch Front and Back pieces at shoulder seam. Neaten raw

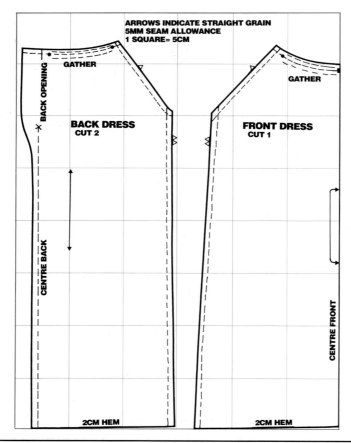

edges and press seam towards back.

Gather Sleeve slightly between notches. Pin and stitch right sides of Sleeve and armhole together. Neaten raw edges, clip curves and press seam towards sleeve.

Place right side of Neck Binding to right side of neck edge. Pin and stitch, matching centre backs.

Fold in centre back ends of Neck Binding. Fold in seam allowance along raw edge of Neck Binding, fold Neck Binding in half over raw edge of neck and slip-stitch in place.

Handstitch press stud to centre back, lapping left side over right side.

Turn Sleeve hem up 1cm, then another 1cm. Stitch, neaten raw edges.

Matching notches and seams, pin and stitch right sides of Sleeve and side seam together. Neaten raw edges.

Machine stitch a narrow hem on lower edge of Sleeves.

OVERALLS FOR BOY BUNNY
50cm x 115cm-wide cotton fabric
14cm x 5mm-wide elastic
2 small press studs
2 buttons
Thread

Cut fabric using pattern. Pattern has 5mm seam allowances.

Place right sides of Pants pieces together, matching centre back notches and centre front notches. Pin and stitch centre front and centre back seams.

Stitch inside leg seams, matching centre seam and notches. Pin right sides of Bib pieces together. Stitch around Bib, leaving seam between notches open. Turn right side out and press.

Fold each Strap in half lengthwise, with right sides together. Stitch along long raw edge, turn right side out and press. Pin one end of each Strap to back of Pants between Xs.

Fold in raw edge of Pants waist, including Straps, and fold again on foldline. Stitch in place to form a casing, leaving an opening between the dots to insert elastic. Secure elastic by stitching each end to Pants waist at dots.

Turn in raw edges of Bib opening and pin Bib to underside of Pants between dots. Topstitch around waist edge securing Bib.

Check Strap lengths on bunny, crossing Straps at back. Trim to correct length. Turn in raw edges of Straps and stitch.

Handstitch press studs to secure Straps to top corners of Bib front. Sew on buttons for decoration.

Machine stitch a narrow hem on lower edges of Pants.

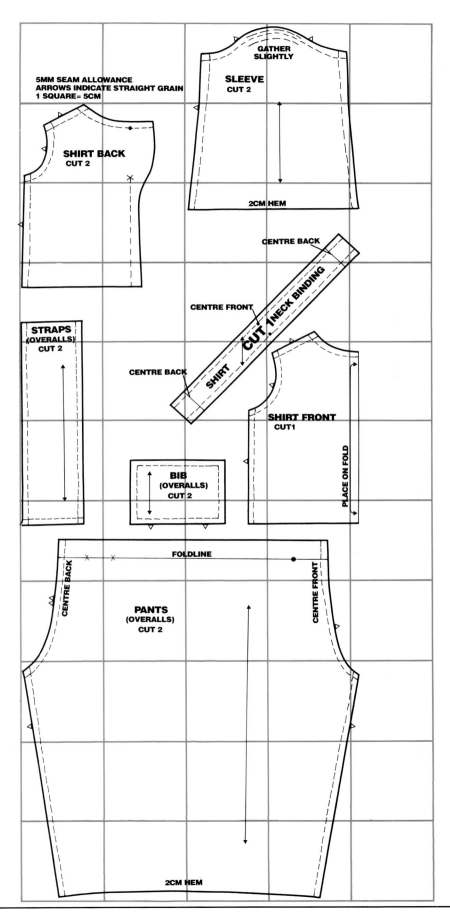

Made by Jenny Manning

Door Mat

Door mat
Stencil film (we used acetate)
Fabric paints, in black and red
Paint brush
Scalpel or craft knife

Enlarge pattern at right following instructions on page 126.

Trace pattern onto stencil film. Cut around outline using knife. Narrow sections of stencil above door, below windows, and at the base of "O" must not be cut through as they hold sections of stencil in place.

Pin stencil to mat. Paint carefully around edges of each cut-out section so paint does not run under stencil, then dab brush into mat firmly to distribute paint evenly. Refer to picture for colours.

Allow paint to dry thoroughly. Fix paint by using a hairdryer to heat painted area for several minutes.

ABOVE: Door Mat.
RIGHT: Silk Handkerchief.

1 SQUARE= 5CM

Silk Handkerchief

Attractive scarves can also be made using this technique and a larger piece of fabric.

30cm square fine silk fabric
Silk dyes (we used Elbesoie, available from craft stores)
Gutta and applicator (available from craft stores)
Small paint brush
Masking tape
Frame (picture frame or silk-screen frame) slightly smaller than fabric
Thread
White tissue paper
Aluminium foil
Steamer or pressure cooker
Vinegar

Stretch fabric across frame, tape fabric to frame along each side (if using a silk-screen, tape fabric to back of frame, not onto screen).

Fill applicator with gutta. Draw design on fabric using applicator. Each separate colour of the design must be surrounded by an unbroken line of gutta. When design is complete, allow gutta to dry.

Dip brush into dye. Lightly touch brush to fabric and dye will spread within gutta outline. Continue to apply a small amount of dye until each section is coloured. (If too much dye is applied it may run over the gutta line and bleed into another section.) When dyeing is complete leave to dry.

To fix dye. Roll dyed fabric in tissue paper. Seal each end of the paper roll by wrapping in aluminium foil. Steam fabric for 1 hour in steamer or pressure cooker containing water with a few drops of vinegar added. (A bamboo steamer in a covered wok is a cheap, efficient alternative to an electric steamer or pressure cooker.)

Using a hot iron, press fabric between tissue paper. Remove paper, stitch a narrow hem along each side of handkerchief.

If gutta has been applied thickly it may have to be removed by dry cleaning. Permanent gutta in metallic colours is also available from specialist craft stores.

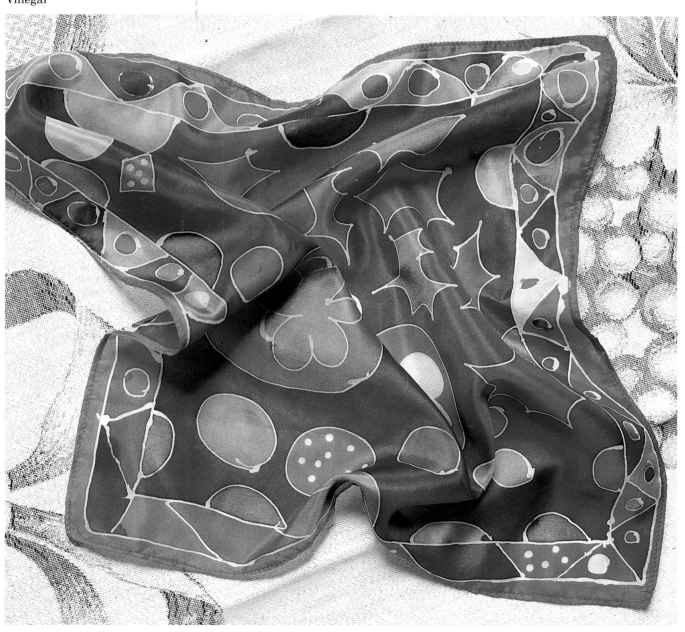

Beads

FOR EACH NECKLACE:
Beads (we used glass and metal beads)
Fine nylon-covered wire (we used
    Tiger Tail, from bead and fishing
    tackle stores), or very strong thread
1 clasp
2 crimps (available from bead and
    craft stores) if using wire
Long nose pliers

Thread one end of wire through crimp
and clasp as shown in diagram below.
Using long nose pliers, crush crimp
onto wire, trim excess wire. If using
thread, attach clasp with a knot instead
of using a crimp.

Thread beads onto wire in pattern of
your choice, to desired length. Attach
crimp and clasp at other end. Crush
crimp onto wire, trim wire.
Note. Nylon-covered wire is sold in
various gauges. Choose a gauge to suit
the size of the hole in the beads.

If making a long strand of beads,
clasp is unnecessary. Thread each end
of wire through a crimp, loop ends
around each other and thread back
through crimp. Complete as above.

BELOW and RIGHT: Beads.

Made by Brooke Cowley

Lingerie Bag

40cm x 115cm-wide nylon organza
    fabric
1.6m ribbon
Assorted silk ribbons for embroidery
    (we used light and medium pink,
    lemon and green)
Water-soluble pen
Six stranded embroidery thread, in
    green
Fine tapestry needle

Size: 30cm x 20cm
Cut 4 pieces of fabric 32cm x 22cm.

Place 2 pieces right sides together,
stitch along one 22cm edge (top) open
out and fold, wrong sides together.
Press. Tack remaining 3 sides together.
Repeat with remaining organza pieces.
These 2 pieces form front and back of
bag.

Trace design at right onto front,
using water-soluble pen and centring
design just above 22cm bottom edge.

Work design through both layers of
fabric, using silk ribbons, in colours of
your choice, and tapestry needle. Work
flower stems using 2 strands of green
thread in stem stitch. See page 124 for

embroidery stitch instructions. Stitch a ribbon bow above flower stems.

Place front over back, right sides together, stitch along 30cm sides and base. Neaten seams and turn right side out.

Stitch around top edge of bag, 4cm and 5.5cm from top edge, to form casing. Make small holes in casing at each side seam on outer fabric only, stitch around holes to neaten.

Cut ribbon into 2 lengths of 75cm. Thread one ribbon through casing from each side of bag (ribbon should enter and exit same hole). Tie ribbon ends into a bow.

BELOW: Lingerie Bag.

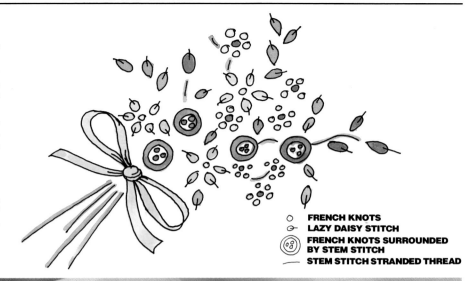

○ FRENCH KNOTS
LAZY DAISY STITCH
FRENCH KNOTS SURROUNDED BY STEM STITCH
STEM STITCH STRANDED THREAD

Made by Jan Evans

Embroidered Door Stop

20cm x 115cm-wide wool flannel (or velvet)
20cm x 115cm-wide calico (for lining)
7 cups clean dry sand, preferably river sand
Tapestry wool in green, deep pink, rose pink, pale pink and maroon
1m cord
Size 20 tapestry needle
Craft glue

Cut two 18cm-diameter circles and one 60cm x 12cm rectangle of flannel. Cut same size pieces of calico. 1cm seam allowance included.

Using tapestry wool and needle, embroider design on one circle of flannel following diagram at right. See page 124 for stitch instructions.

LAZY DAISY STITCH

STEM STITCH

FRENCH KNOT

WOOL ROSES

Made by From Lois with Love (02) 969 6847 (classes available)

Made by Jenny Manning

LEFT: Embroidered Door Stop.
ABOVE: Sewing Set.

Work French knots for small buds; lazy daisy stitch for 5 petalled flowers and leaves; stem stitch for stems. Work wool roses by stitching a square of 4 satin stitches surrounded with stem stitches.

Embroidery colours. Use deep pink for the centre square and rose pink then pale pink for the surrounding stem stitches. Use olive green for stems, leaf green for leaves. Use pale pink and maroon for small buds, rose pink for 5 petalled flowers. Use pale pink for 3 lazy daisy petals next to large roses.

To assemble. Stitch one long side of rectangular piece of flannel (wall) around edge of embroidered flannel circle, right sides together. Stitch second flannel circle to the other long edge of the wall, leaving narrow ends of wall open. Turn right side out.

Repeat with calico pieces but do not turn right side out. Insert calico lining into flannel case through opening in wall. Position lining inside door stop and fill lining with sand.

Handstitch lining closed with firm stitches, then handstitch flannel case closed.

Glue cord around top seam of door stop. Tie a cord bow and glue onto cord where ends meet.

Sewing Set

PINCUSHION
Heart-shaped balsa wood box
20cm x 90cm-wide cotton fabric
10cm x 90cm-wide calico fabric
50cm ribbon, same width as box
   height
Craft glue
Polyester fibre filling
Pegs or paper clips
Small piece of stiff cardboard
Thread

Note. We used a box with a 33cm perimeter. Increase fabric amounts if box is larger.

Place box on cotton fabric and trace

around it. Cut fabric 1cm larger all around than box, glue to base. Clip V-shapes from excess fabric, glue to box sides as shown in diagram below.

Cut a strip of fabric 4cm-wide and long enough to fit perimeter of box. Fold strip in half lengthways, wrong sides together, press. Glue strip over top edge of box, placing folded edge on box rim and overlapping ends.

Cut a calico strip slightly narrower than ribbon and long enough to fit perimeter of box. Cut ribbon to fit box perimeter. Glue calico to side of box to ensure a smooth surface for ribbon.

Glue ribbon over calico, overlapping ends neatly. Hold in place with pegs or paper clips until dry.

Trace two more fabric hearts onto cotton fabric using box as a pattern. Cut fabric 2cm larger all around than box. Place hearts right sides together and stitch, leaving 1cm seam allowance and a 6cm opening on one side. Turn right side out, press. Fill with polyester fibre, handstitch opening closed.

To make heart-shaped button in centre, cut a small heart from cardboard. Pierce two holes in centre of heart using a large needle. Cut cotton fabric 5mm larger all around than cardboard piece. Glue fabric to cardboard, clip V-shapes from excess fabric as with box base, and glue excess to back of heart.

Using double thread, take a few stitches through pincushion centre and tugging thread to make slight indentation. Stitch button in place, passing needle through holes previously made in cardboard. Glue pin cushion into box. Cut a tiny fabric heart and glue over button centre.

SCISSOR HOLDER
20cm x 90cm-wide cotton fabric
30cm x 4cm-wide ribbon
Thick cardboard
Craft glue
Pegs or paper clips

Make patterns by tracing over actual size diagrams below. Cut the 3 pieces from cardboard. Cut 3 pieces 1cm larger all around than cardboard pieces, from fabric.

Glue each cardboard piece to fabric, clip V-shapes out of excess fabric on Front and Back glue excess to back of Front and Back. See instructions for Pincushion. Glue excess fabric to back of Half Front along straight edge only.

Glue a ribbon strip across straight edge of Half Front and down centre of Front as pictured.

Place Half Front piece, right side down on table. Place scissors on Half Front and position right side of Front piece on top of scissors. Run a line of glue around bottom half of Front, on back. Glue excess fabric from curved portions of Half Front onto back of Front. Hold in place with pegs or paper clips until dry.

Run a line of glue around back of Front and glue Back onto Front, wrong sides together. Hold pieces together with paper clips or pegs until dry.

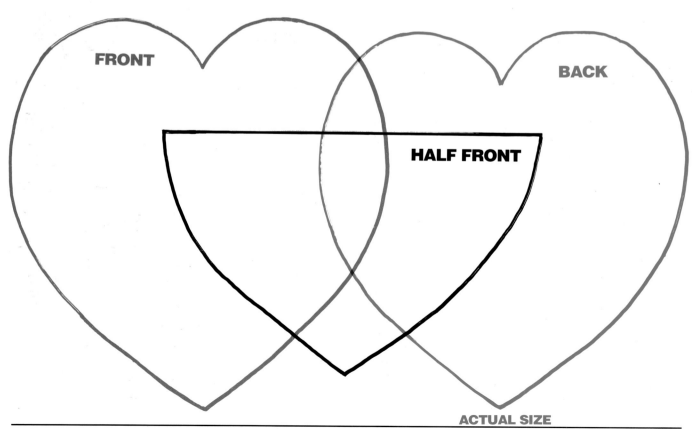

FRONT

BACK

HALF FRONT

ACTUAL SIZE

Made by Rosa Alonso

Nappy Pincushion

20cm x 90cm-wide fine linen or cotton
   fabric
60cm x 2.5cm-wide gathered lace
Silk embroidery ribbon, in 3 shades
   each of pink, blue, yellow, and 2
   shades of green
Six stranded embroidery thread, in
   green
No.20 tapestry needle
Polyester fibre filling

Cut 2 rectangles of fabric 16cm x 11cm.
1cm seam allowance is included.

Position centre three roses of
embroidery design about 4.5cm away
from bottom left corner of one fabric
piece. Work design following diagram
at right. See page 124 for embroidery
stitch instructions.

Work 1-3 French knots for rose
centres in darkest shade of pink, blue
or yellow ribbon. Surround centre with
a row of stem stitch in medium shade of
same colour ribbon. Keep stem stitch
tension loose and work carefully so
stem stitches curve around French
knots to make petals. Work another
row of stem stitch around first row, in
lightest shade of same colour ribbon.

Work rosebuds in lazy daisy stitch
using pink, blue or yellow ribbon. Make
one lazy daisy stitch in medium shade;
re-work holding stitch in dark shade of
same colour.

Work small single roses using one
French knot in pink, blue or yellow.

Work leaves by making one lazy
daisy stitch for each leaf, using dark or
light green ribbon as desired.

Work stems in backstitch using one
strand of green embroidery thread.

Tips. Work with about 40cm of ribbon
at a time. If ribbon twists, drop needle
and allow ribbon to untwist.

To thread needle, cut end of ribbon
diagonally.

To assemble pincushion. Pin lace
around embroidered fabric piece, right
sides together and with scalloped edge
of lace towards centre of fabric. Tack
lace to fabric, join ends of lace neatly
with French seam.

Pin fabric pieces (cushion front and
back) right sides together. Stitch front
to back using 6mm seam allowance and
making two diagonal stitches across
each corner. Leave an opening on one
side. Trim corners and seam allowance,
turn cushion right side out.

Fill with polyester fibre, stitch opening closed.

✿	**FRENCH KNOT**
➴	**LAZY DAISY STITCH**
➶	**LAZY DAISY ROSEBUD**
⊛	**FRENCH KNOTS SURROUNDED BY STEM STITCH**
⌒	**STEM STITCH**

Made by Jennifer Pagewood

Cross-Stitch Miniatures

3 x 20cm squares 14-count Aida fabric
DMC six stranded embroidery thread
  (see key for colours, one skein each
  colour)
Tapestry needle

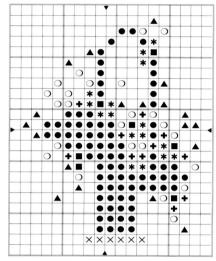

		DMC No.
Frame	Mid green	989
✕	Brown	356
●	Coffee	758
■	Deep pink	335
✱	Pink	899
✚	Pale pink	894
○	Green	3364
▲	Pale green	772

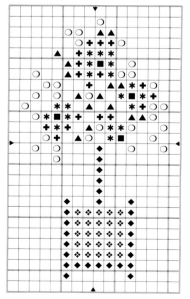

		DMC No.
■	Magenta	917
✱	Rose pink	3607
✚	Dusty pink	3608
◆	Dark green	3347
❖	Mid green	989
○	Green	3364
▲	Pale green	772

Work cross-stitch using 3 strands of thread and backstitch using 2 strands. See page 124 for embroidery stitch instructions.

Position design in centre of fabric square. Each symbol represents one cross-stitch embroidered over one fabric square. Each design has a graph with separate key.

When cross-stitch is complete, work a backstitch frame in mid green (989) around design, one square from outside edge of design. Work a single cross-stitch outside each corner of frame in same colour.

Press from the wrong side on a padded surface.

Completed embroideries should be professionally framed.

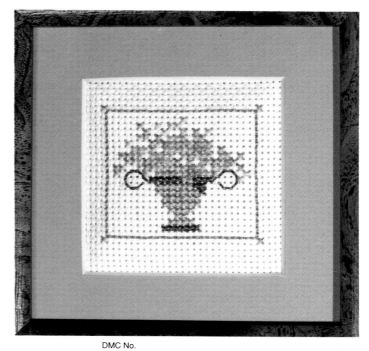

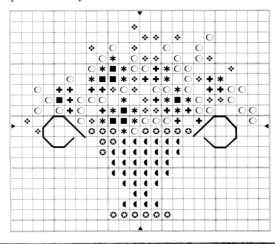

		DMC No.
✪	Dark Blue	930
❯	Blue	932
❖	Mid green	989
○	Green	3347
■	Rust	3328
✱	Apricot	3341
✚	Coffee	758
❙	Dark blue (backstitch)	930

LEFT, ABOVE and BELOW: Cross-Stitch Miniatures.

Left: Lamp: From Lois with Love

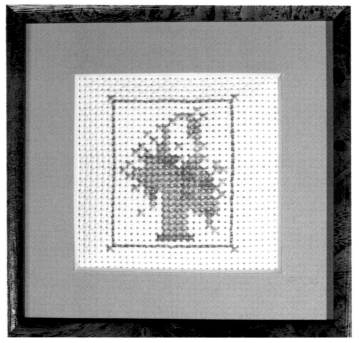

Made by Jenny Manning

Rainbow Petticoat

1.2m x 115cm-wide taffeta fabric
1m x 140cm-wide tulle to match
  taffeta
6 strips 20cm x 140cm-wide tulle, in
  different colours
50cm x 2cm-wide elastic
Dressmaker's pencil

Size: 8-10 years old

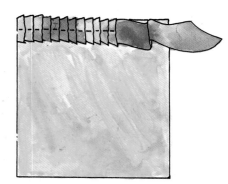

Note. Tulle is difficult to pin. When sewing pieces of tulle together, it is best to hold fabric firmly in place rather than pin.

Cut 2 pieces of taffeta, 115cm x 45cm and 2 pieces of matching tulle, 115cm x 45cm for Skirt. 1cm seam allowances are included.

Place taffeta Skirt pieces right sides together, pin and stitch along 45cm side seams. Turn back a 2.5cm hem along bottom edge, pin and stitch.

Place tulle Skirt pieces together, stitch 45cm side using narrow zigzag stitch.

Cut 2 taffeta rectangles, 38cm x 17cm for Skirt Yoke. Place right sides together, pin and stitch along 17cm sides; press. Turn back a 3cm casing along top edge, pin and stitch, leaving a small opening to insert elastic.

Cut coloured tulle into 20cm x 10cm rectangles (we used about 50 rectangles). Stitch together along 10cm sides into a continuous strip, alternating colours. Stitch ends of strip together, fold into quarters, mark quarters with pencil.

Fold tulle Skirt into quarters, mark quarters along hem with pencil. Place tulle strip over bottom of tulle Skirt, raw edges together. Matching chalk marks on Skirt and strip, stitch strip to Skirt along centre of strip, gathering or pleating the strip to fit while stitching. See diagram at left.

Place tulle Skirt over taffeta Skirt so top edges match. Gather both layers together using longest machine stitch and stitching 8mm and 3mm from top edge.

Pin Skirt to Skirt Yoke, right sides together, matching side seams and adjusting gathers to fit. Stitch and neaten seam.

Insert elastic through casing, stitch elastic ends together, stitch opening closed. Turn right side out.

Marble Bag

48cm x 22cm corduroy fabric
10cm square of fusible webbing
Bright fabric scraps (for applique)
Threads to match corduroy and each
    applique fabric
4 large wooden beads
50cm cord

Press corduroy in half, across width, wrong sides together.

For marbles. Fuse small scraps of fabric onto webbing. Trace circles on fabric using coins as a pattern. Cut out as many as desired. Fuse marbles to corduroy, positioning them just above foldline on one side of bag only.

Stitch around each marble using a close zigzag stitch and matching thread.

Fold bag in half, right sides together. Stitch sides together using 1cm seam allowance and leaving a 1cm gap, on one side, 6cm from top to thread cord through.

Neaten top raw edge of bag. Fold 4cm of top edge of bag to outside. Pin and stitch 3.5cm from fold. Pin and stitch again 2cm from fold. Turn bag right side out and press.

Thread cord through casing, thread two beads onto each end and knot cord ends together.

LEFT: Rainbow Petticoat.
BELOW: Marble Bag.

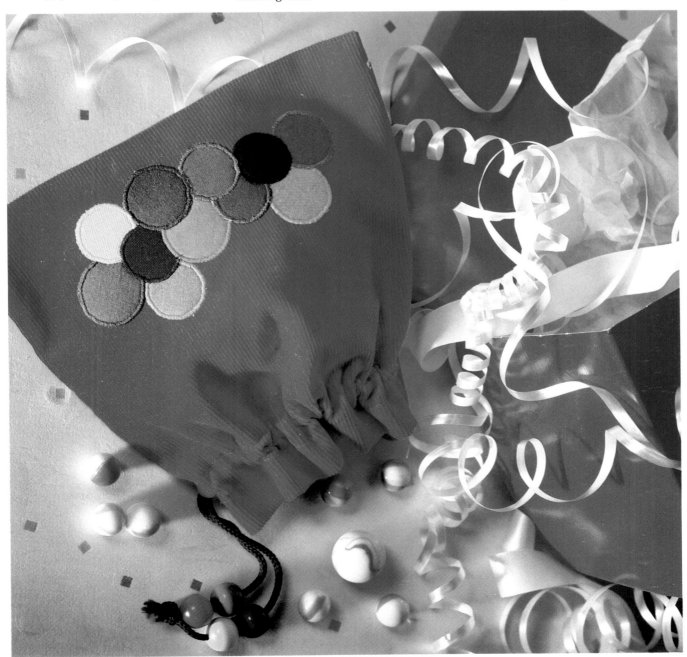

Made by Jenny Manning

NATURAL TOUCHES

Fragrant flowers, herbs and fruit have long been used in beauty treatments to refresh, cleanse, soothe and enhance the complexion. We have included a variety of totally natural mixtures which will make fabulous gifts for anyone who enjoys being pampered. Our cosmetics have a relatively short shelf life because they do not contain any preservatives, so store them in a cool place.

Peppermint Bath Sachets

25cm muslin
1½ cups dried peppermint leaves
3m ribbon

Cut muslin into 12 x 10cm circles. Place 2 tablespoonfuls of peppermint leaves into centre of each circle, gather edges together to enclose leaves and secure with 50cm ribbon. Tie ribbon into a bow, knot ends of ribbon to enable sachet to be hung under a running tap.
Makes about 12 sachets.

Rose Geranium and Lavender Massage Oil

¼ cup rose geranium petals
¼ cup lavender
1 cup apricot oil

Place petals in a glass jar. Gently warm apricot oil in saucepan on very low heat, pour over petals, seal. Leave in a warm place for 2 weeks, shaking jar each day. Warm oil slightly in saucepan on very low heat, strain through muslin, discard petals; pour into bottles, seal. For a more pungent perfume, repeat using fresh petals.
Makes about 1 cup.

LEFT: Rose Geranium and Lavender Massage Oil.
BELOW: Peppermint Bath Sachets.

Left: Bottle, tassels: Home and Garden. Basket, cloth, towel, wreath: Balmain Linen and Lace. Below: Wreath, cushion: Balmain Linen and Lace. Cloth: Home and Garden

Avocado Body Cream

10g beeswax
¼ cup avocado oil
6 drops jasmine oil
2 tablespoons rosewater
¼ teaspoon borax

Gently heat beeswax, avocado oil and jasmine oil in top of a double saucepan over simmering water. Stir until beeswax melts and mixture is smooth, remove from heat. Blend rosewater and borax together, stir into beeswax mixture. Stir until mixture has cooled, place into a jar, seal.

Makes about ¼ cup.

Orange Flower Body Lotion

Chill this lotion for a soothing effect on sunburn.

⅓ cup orange flower water
2 tablespoons glycerine

Whisk orange flower water and glycerine together in small bowl, pour into a small bottle, seal. Shake well before using.

Makes about 1 small bottle.

LEFT: Avocado Body Cream
ABOVE: Orange Flower Body Lotion.

Left: Mirror, plate: Mosmania. Frame, jar, bracelet, lingerie: Sandy de Beyer. Towel: Lois with Love. Brush: Flossoms. Above: Jug, tassel: Sandy de Beyer. Basket: Country Form

Marigold Oil

This oil is wonderful for dry skin, add to bathwater or massage into dry hands or feet.

1 cup marigold petals
1 cup almond oil

Place marigold petals in a glass jar, pour almond oil onto petals, seal. Stand on a sunny window sill or in a warm place for 3 weeks, shaking jar each day. Heat oil and petals in small saucepan on medium heat until petals become crisp. Strain through wire strainer lined with muslin or a clean tea-towel, discard petals; pour into bottles, seal.
  Makes about 1 cup.

Honeysuckle Foot Balm

⅓ cup lanolin
3 tablespoons almond oil
3 tablespoons glycerine
¼ teaspoon honeysuckle oil

Place lanolin, almond oil and glycerine in top of a double saucepan over simmering water, stir until evenly combined and smooth. Add honeysuckle oil, remove from heat, continue stirring until cool; pour into small jars, seal.
  Makes about ½ cup.

Spicy Splash-On

5 cinnamon sticks
1 tablespoon cloves
1 litre boiling water
2 tablespoons vodka

Place cinnamon and cloves in a glass jar, pour in boiling water, allow to cool slightly. Add vodka, stir, seal. Allow to steep for 2 days; strain, discard spices; pour liquid into bottles, seal.
  Makes about 1 litre.

LEFT: Marigold Oil.
ABOVE RIGHT: Honeysuckle Foot Balm.
RIGHT: Spicy Splash-On.

Left: Bottle: Home and Garden. Cushion: Belinda's Corner Shop. Basket, cage, print: Balmain Linen and Lace. Above right: Tissue box, towel: Lois with Love. Bowl: Flossoms. Bowls: Sandy de Beyer. Right: Mirror: Sandy de Beyer. Photographs: Flossoms. Wooden tray: Country Form

Floral Toilet Water

Refreshing and pleasantly fragrant, floral scented water works wonders when lightly sprayed over a hot or tired body. Keep in a cool place away from direct light.

2 cups fresh flower petals (roses, freesias, lavender, violets or a mixture of fragrant flower petals)
1 litre boiling water
2 tablespoons vodka

Fill a glass jar with flower petals, cover petals with boiling water, allow to cool slightly. Stir in vodka, cover, allow to cool; strain through muslin, discard petals; pour liquid into bottles, seal.
   Makes about 1 litre.

Rose Petal Bath Oil

1 cup fresh rose petals
1½ cups sunflower oil

Pack rose petals into a glass jar. Gently warm oil in saucepan on very low heat, pour over petals, seal. Stand in a sunny place for 2 weeks, shaking each day. Warm oil slightly in saucepan on very low heat; strain through a double layer of muslin, discard petals; pour oil into bottles, seal.
   Makes about 1½ cups.

BELOW: Floral Toilet Water.
RIGHT: Rose Petal Bath Oil.
FAR RIGHT: Chamomile Hand Cream.

Below: Large print and bowl: Country Form. Small print: Sandy de Beyer. Right: Hat: Belinda's Corner Shop. Cushion, tray, make-up bag and bangle: Les Olivades. Bottle: Home and Garden. Far right: Tray, jug, towel, bowl: Balmain Linen and Lace. Small dish: Belinda's Corner Shop

Chamomile Hand Cream

Chamomile is believed to soften and whiten hands.
To prepare chamomile infusion, pour boiling water over ¼ cup chamomile flowers, allow to steep until cool; strain and use as required.

1 tablespoon cocoa butter
¼ cup vitamin E cream
3 tablespoons strong chamomile
 infusion

Gently melt cocoa butter in small saucepan on low heat. Remove from heat and allow to cool slightly. Whisk in vitamin E cream and the chamomile infusion; continue to whisk until mixture cools and begins to thicken. Pour into jar, seal.

 Makes about ¼ cup.

Floral Bath Sachets

The oatmeal in these sachets will help soften water for a soothing bath. It is best to use dry petals if you require the sachets to be kept for more than 3 days.

50cm muslin
½ cup fresh or dried flower petals
 (lavender, rose, jasmine and/or
 marigold)
3 tablespoons oatmeal
4m ribbon

Cut muslin into 18cm x 8cm rectangles. Fold rectangles in half and sew along two edges to form a pocket. Fill each bag with petals and a little oatmeal. Secure with 50cm of ribbon, tie into a bow. Knot ends of ribbon to enable sachet to be hung under a running tap.
 Makes about 20 sachets.

Herb Scented Water

1 bunch lemon thyme
1 bunch rosemary
2 tablespoons violets
1 litre boiling water
2 tablespoons vodka
1 drop green food colouring

Place thyme, rosemary and violets in a glass jar, pour boiling water over herbs, allow to cool slightly. Add vodka and colouring; stir and seal. Allow to stand for 1 week, shaking jar each day. Strain through wire strainer lined with muslin or a clean tea-towel, discard petals and herbs; pour liquid into bottles, seal.
 Makes about 1 litre.

BELOW: Floral Bath Sachets.
RIGHT: Herb Scented Water.

Below: All accessories: Balmain Linen and Lace.
Right: Bowl and cushion: Balmain Linen and Lace.
Frame, bottle, handkerchief, cloth: Home and Garden

Photography: Andre Martin

Styling: Michelle Gorry

Made by From Lois with Love (02) 969 6847 (classes available)

FROM THE GARDEN

A wreath of brilliant colour, a delicate lace hanky filled with your favourite potpourri, a sweet scented lavender ribbon sachet or a pot of fresh herbs are just a few of the wonderful gift ideas that follow.

Scented Topiary Tree

Plaster of Paris
Small terracotta pot
Plasticine or clay
40cm x 1cm-diameter dowel rod
9cm-diameter Oasis ball (from florists)
4m x 3cm-wide ribbon
20 x 20cm fine florists' wires
Dried and artificial flowers (including natural seed pods, lavender heads, hydrangeas and rose buds)
⅓ cup potpourri or dried lavender
Wire cutters

Mix small quantity of plaster following manufacturer's instructions. Place plasticine or clay ball into base of pot, pour Plaster of Paris into pot until 3cm from top.

Centre rod upright in pot; push into plasticine. Check rod remains centred as plaster sets; allow the plaster to set hard.

Centre Oasis ball above rod, push down gently until rod is about halfway through ball.

Cut ribbon into 7 x 45cm pieces. Tie each piece into a bow, twist wire around centre of each bow, trim wire stem to 3cm using wire cutters.

Wire any fragile flower stems as shown in diagram on page 59, trim wires to 3cm. Stronger stems do not need to be wired and can be pushed directly into Oasis ball. Make sure all flower stems are of even length so topiary is balanced.

Gently push flower stems into ball, working around ball, fill all gaps. Tie large bow around dowel at base of ball.

Cover plaster with potpourri or lavender, scatter with left-over flower heads. A ribbon bow can be tied and glued around top of pot, if desired.

Victorian Posy

Posies were originally carried to ward off evil spirits and to promote health. During Victorian times they became more decorative and often contained flowers which conveyed a special message, such as forget-me-nots which symbolise true love.

Fresh flowers (we used miniature rosebuds, hyacinths, lavender, jonquils, violets and violet leaves)
Florists' wire
Ribbon

Arrange posy in your hand, take one rosebud for the centre and surround it with a row of rosebuds. Build posy by adding rows of hyacinth, lavender, rosebuds, jonquils and violets until posy is desired size.

Complete with a row of violet leaves, twist wire firmly around posy stems to keep flowers in place; tie with ribbon.

LEFT: Scented Topiary Tree.
BELOW: Victorian Posy.

Left: Birdcage: Balmain Linen and Lace. Below: Tapestry cushion: Balmain Linen and Lace

Made by Bloomey's

Made by Bloomey's

Fresh Floral Wreath

Fresh flowers (we used roses, daffodils, daisy chrysanthemums, alstroemerias, wattle, tiger lillies, jonquils, freesias, heath, cotoneaster, lavender)
Florists' wire
Polystyrene wreath base (from florists)
Wire cutters

Wire stems as shown in box below, leaving about 4cm of wire below each stem.

Push wires of large flowers into polystyrene base around top of wreath. Add more large flowers to inside centre of wreath.

Fill gaps with leafy stems and smaller flowers. Continue until wreath base is covered.

Made by Bloomey's

Fresh Herb Posy

Fresh herbs (we used flowering mint, varieties of mint leaves, lavender flowers and leaves, rosemary, parsley and thyme)
String

Arrange posy in your hand, take a bunch of herbs for the centre and surround it with a mixed row of herbs. Build posy by adding rows of herbs and herb flowers until posy is desired size.

Complete with a row of parsley, tie string firmly around posy stems to keep herbs in place.

WIRING FLOWER STEMS
Wiring is sometimes necessary to strengthen a brittle stem or to reinforce a stem which is to be pushed into polystyrene. Trim stems and bend the wire almost in half. Position wire behind stem and twist one leg of wire twice around stem and other wire leg as shown in diagram. Bend wire end down in line with other wire.

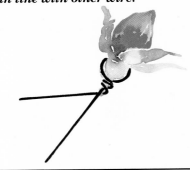

LEFT: Fresh Herb Posy.
ABOVE: Fresh Floral Wreath.

Made by Bloomey's

Lavender Bottles

Lavender heads with stems at least
   12cm long
String

Take a bunch of about 14 lavender
heads, tie together with string under
flower heads. Wind string around
flower heads, tie to secure; leave
lavender overnight to allow stems to
wilt. Bring stems up and over flower
heads, spacing them evenly apart.

   Tie together with string at top of
flower heads, trim stalk ends.

   Hang by strings in a warm, dry place
out of direct sunlight until dry.

ABOVE: Lavender Bottles.

Herb Pots

Terracotta pots
Potting mix
Herb seedlings

Plan beforehand to grow herb pots in time for gift giving. Fill pots with potting mix, plant the herb seedlings. Fertilise, keep well watered and pinch off tips to encourage bushier growth until you have a well established plant.

Give copies of your favourite herb recipes with herb pots.

A Box of Bouquet Garni

Adding a bouquet garni to a soup, casserole or stock is a traditional way of seasoning and enhancing the flavour of home cooked dishes. Each recipe makes enough for one bouquet garni, multiply quantities as required. Make a boxful for a keen cook and include a favourite recipe.

CLASSIC BOUQUET GARNI
1 teaspoon parsley flakes
¼ teaspoon dried thyme leaves
1 bay leaf

FOR POULTRY
1 teaspoon dried tarragon leaves
1 teaspoon dried oregano leaves
1 bay leaf
1 teaspoon whole black peppercorns

FOR SEAFOOD
1 teaspoon dried tarragon leaves
1 teaspoon dried basil leaves
¼ teaspoon dried dill leaf tips
1 bay leaf

Combine herbs and place in 15cm-diameter circle of muslin or cheese-cloth. Secure tightly with long piece of string to form a sachet.

LEFT: Bouquet Garni.
ABOVE: Herb Pots.

Above: Watering-can and fork: Duane Norris Garden Designers

ABOVE: Pots of
Colour.
RIGHT: Fruit
Box.
FAR RIGHT: Ivy
Wreath.

Pots of Colour

Geraniums and succulents such as zygocactus and burro's tail will propagate easily from a cutting. Cut a stem section with a clean sharp knife, plant in good quality potting mix and water well.

Make sure the plant is well established before giving it away. Decorate the pot with a large ribbon bow.

Fruit or Vegetable Box

Decorative packages of fruit or vegetables make a delicious and nutritious treat for fruit lovers or hard-to-buy-for grandparents.

Use only the choicest in-season fruit or vegetables from your garden or local fruit market. Present it boxed beautifully with cellophane lining and a ribbon bow.

Ivy Wreath

Long ivy stems
Limes (flowers can be used instead)
Florists' wire
Ribbon

Take two long ivy strands, wire together at cut ends as pictured.

Shape ivy into a circle, twist remaining ends around each other to form a wreath. Twist wire around wreath at intervals to keep ivy in place.

Continue twisting ivy around wreath until desired thickness, securing with wire if necessary.

Push wire through limes or twist wire around flower stems as shown in diagram on page 59. Twist wire ends around wreath to secure limes or flowers.

Tie a ribbon bow at top of wreath.

DRYING FLOWERS

Dried flowers can be used in many crafts to make pretty and lasting floral gifts. The aim is to remove moisture from the blooms while maintaining their shape and colour. Drying time will vary depending on size and moisture content of flowers. There are several methods which can be used.

Hang Drying

Strip excess leaves, tie in small bunches using a rubber band. Hang upside down in a warm, dry place where air can circulate around the bunch. Avoid direct sunlight and dust. By hanging bunches upside down, flower heads remain upright.

Drying in Silica Gel

Flowers dried properly in silica gel will retain their bright colour and fresh appearance. When dry, silica gel is blue; as it becomes moist, the colour is lost and it turns pink or white. To reuse, place silica gel on a flat oven tray in very a slow oven for about 30 minutes or until it turns blue again. Silica gel is available from pharmacies and craft stores.

To dry flowers, pour a layer of silica gel into an airtight container. Place flowers face up in silica gel, gently push until flowers are half in silica. (If blossoms are flat or small they can be

Drying flowers in silica gel.

placed face down.) Gently cover flowers with silica gel, making sure grains fill inside of flowers; this helps hold their original shape. Seal container, place in a warm, dry cupboard.

Check flowers every day, when flowers are ready they will feel papery and dry. If left in silica too long, the petals will break up. If flowers are to be used in wreaths it is easier to insert wires into stems before drying.

Once flowers are dry, remove from

silica gel and gently brush away remaining grains.

Roses, lilies, daffodils and peonies are some of the flowers suitable for drying in silica gel.

Microwave Drying

Many flowers can be successfully dried in the microwave. The colour will change slightly during drying.

Choose flowers with half-open petals. Thick petal flowers such as pansies, roses, carnations, gypsophila and chrysanthemums will give the best results.

Method 1. Cut stems below the bud, half fill a microwave safe bowl with fine silica gel (available from pharmacies and craft stores). Place flowers face up, gently push until flowers are half in silica. Sprinkle silica gel between petals. Microwave on HIGH for 1 minute, if petals are still soft, microwave on HIGH for 30 seconds at a time until dry. Brush silica from top of flowers, stand flowers for several minutes to cool.

Method 2. Strip away foliage, place a single layer of flowers between several layers of kitchen towels, microwave on HIGH for about 3 minutes or until dry. Replace paper if wet; stand flowers for several minutes to cool.

Everlasting Wreath

Flowers and foliage which can be
dried (we used silver dollar gum,
statice, sea lavender and peonies)
Grape-vine wreath (from florists or
decorator stores)
Florists' wire
Ribbon

Wrap ribbon around wreath and knot
ends together.

BELOW: Everlasting Wreath.
FAR RIGHT: Dried Flower Wreath.

Arrange flowers in your hand starting with a large bloom such as a peony, then add statice, sea lavender and gum stems.

Twist wire around bunch and wire bunch to wreath next to ribbon knot.

Wire a second bunch on opposite

side of knot; add a smaller bunch between the first two, adjust flowers to cover wire.

Tie a ribbon bow at top of wreath.

Dried Flower Wreath

Dried flowers (we used hydrangeas, everlasting daisies, babies breath, peonies, cornflowers, lichen and delphinium, see notes on drying flowers on page 63)
Silk flowers (optional)
Straw wreath (from florists or decorator stores)
Ribbon
Craft glue (a hot glue gun would be useful)

Attach large dried and silk flowers to wreath by gluing or pushing stems into wreath. Brittle stems should be wired; see diagram on page 59.

Fill spaces between large flowers with sprays of babies breath, hydrangea and small flowers.

Tie a ribbon bow and wire onto wreath at base.

Ribbon Lavender Sachets

30-35cm ribbon, at least 3cm-wide, for each bag
Narrow ribbon or cord
Dried lavender
Thread

Fold ribbon in half across width, right sides together; stitch side seams close to edge. Turn sachet right side out, push out corners; cut across raw ribbon ends with pinking shears.

Fill with lavender, tie with narrow ribbon or cord to make a bow.

Alternatively, for narrow ribbon, fold ribbon in half across width, wrong sides together. Stitch sides together close to edge. Complete as above.

ABOVE: Ribbon Lavender Sachets.
ABOVE RIGHT: Lacy Scented Sachets.
RIGHT: Fresh Herb Wreath.

Above right: Box: Balmain Linen and Lace
Photography: Rodney Weidland

Lacy Scented Sachets

Lace-edged handkerchiefs
Potpourri
Narrow ribbon

Place potpourri in centre of each handkerchief. Bring handkerchief corners together and tie sachet with ribbon.

Fresh Herb Wreath

Fresh herbs (we used mint, parsley and lavender flowers)
Florists' wire
Polystyrene wreath base (from florists)
Felt pen
Ribbon

Trim herb stems. Wire small bunches of herbs; see diagram on page 59.

Mark wreath base into thirds, draw a curved line to divide each section.
Push wired bunches of parsley into wreath base along one curved line.

Add a second row of parsley following curve of first row. Repeat for remaining two curves.
Complete wreath by adding two rows of lavender next to parsley rows, then two rows of mint. Fill spaces with extra herb bunches. Tie ribbon bow at top of wreath.
Herb wreath can be dried by hanging in a warm, dry place out of direct sunlight. If you intend drying the wreath, pack the bunches of herbs closely together as they will shrink and leave spaces.

Made by Bloomey's

SWEET IDEAS

Handmade sweets make simply delicious gifts and in this chapter you'll find something to suit everyone's taste. Choose from wickedly rich chocolate truffles and almond splinters, refreshing jellies, crunchy peanut brittle, creamy honey nougat and much more. Be patient, sweet making requires a little practice and attention to detail so don't rush it.

Before You Start
When making sweets it is important that sugar syrups are cooked to exactly the right temperature. If you do not have a sweets thermometer you can test for "hard crack" stage by dropping half a teaspoon of syrup into a cup of cold water. If the syrup is cooked properly it should set, forming brittle threads that remain brittle when removed from the water. "Soft crack" stage is tested for in the same way – the difference is that the threads are slightly more flexible than they are at hard crack stage. Choose a fine, sunny day to work with sugar syrups as moisture in the air will alter the outcome.

Caramels

125g butter
2 tablespoons golden syrup
1½ cups sugar
400g can sweetened condensed milk
½ cup water
¼ teaspoon cream of tartar
1 teaspoon vanilla essence

Place all ingredients, except essence, in saucepan, stir over low heat until mixture is a pale brown colour (a little mixture dropped into cold water should form a firm but pliable ball). Remove from heat, stir in essence, drop teaspoonfuls of mixture onto greased oven trays; cool. Wrap caramels in cellophane when cold. Store in a cool, dry place.
   Makes about 40.

RIGHT: Caramels.

Lime Jellies

1¼ cups sugar
⅔ cup cold water
2 tablespoons gelatine
¼ cup hot water
½ teaspoon lime flavouring
1 teaspoon green colouring
Castor sugar

Grease and line bar pan with foil. Place sugar and cold water in small saucepan, stir over gentle heat until sugar is dissolved. Brush sides of pan with a wet pastry brush to dissolve sugar crystals. Increase heat and cook until syrup reaches 116°C when tested with a sweets thermometer or until syrup forms a soft ball when tested in a cup of cold water.

Dissolve gelatine in hot water. Add gelatine, flavouring and colouring to syrup, stir quickly until combined, pour into prepared pan. Allow to cool and set; cut jellies into pieces using a wet knife. Toss each jelly in a little castor sugar; store in airtight container.

Makes about 20.

Chocolate Fruit Balls

125g dried apricots, chopped
⅓ cup raisins, chopped
⅓ cup sultanas, chopped
2 teaspoons grated orange rind
60g dark chocolate, grated
180g dark chocolate, extra
60g butter

Combine apricots, raisins, sultanas, rind and grated dark chocolate in small bowl. Roll teaspoons of mixture into balls, refrigerate overnight.

Break extra chocolate into pieces, place in top of a double saucepan with butter over simmering water. Stir until smooth or microwave on HIGH for 2 minutes. Dip each fruit ball in chocolate until evenly coated. Place balls on foil-covered trays; allow to set in a cool place. Store balls in airtight container in refrigerator.

Makes about 25.

Almond Splinters

250g milk chocolate, broken into pieces
150g slivered almonds, toasted

Melt chocolate in top of a double saucepan over simmering water. Stir until smooth or microwave on HIGH for 2 minutes. Combine almonds and chocolate, drop tablespoonfuls of mixture onto foil-covered trays. Allow to set in a cool place; store in airtight container in cool place.

Makes about 25.

LEFT: Lime Jellies.
BELOW: From top: Chocolate Fruit Balls, Almond Splinters.

Lollipops

Lollipops are best made on the day you wish to serve them.

1 cup light corn syrup
1 cup water
2 cups sugar
Flavouring
Colouring
Lollipop sticks

Place corn syrup, water and sugar in small saucepan, stir over low heat until sugar is dissolved. Brush sides of pan with a wet pastry brush to dissolve sugar crystals. Increase heat, cook until syrup reaches 150°C when tested with a sweets thermometer or until syrup reaches hard crack stage. Remove from heat, add a little flavouring and colouring to syrup, stir through. Pour spoonfuls of mixture in desired shapes onto foil-covered trays. Press a lollipop stick into each shape; allow lollipops to cool at room temperature.
Makes about 10.

Flavouring & Colouring Suggestions

For one batch of syrup add ½ teaspoon of raspberry, orange, lime or lemon flavouring and ½ teaspoon of red, orange green or yellow colouring. Mixture can also be divided and flavoured and coloured, as desired, to create multicoloured lollipops.

Chocolate Truffles

⅓ cup thickened cream
150g dark chocolate
30g butter
1 tablespoon brandy
¼ cup cocoa, sifted

Place cream in a small saucepan, bring to the boil. Reduce heat, stir in chocolate until melted, stir in butter and brandy; refrigerate overnight. Roll teaspoons of mixture into balls, dust with cocoa. Refrigerate in airtight container until required.
    Makes about 24.

FAR LEFT: Lollipops.
LEFT: Chocolate Truffles.
ABOVE: Butterscotch.
Above: Boxes: Remo

Butterscotch

½ cup water
3 cups sugar
½ teaspoon cream of tartar
30g butter

Place water in saucepan, bring to the boil. Remove from heat, stir in sugar until dissolved. Return to heat, cover, bring to the boil. Mix cream of tartar with a little water, add to mixture, boil, covered, for 2 minutes. Remove lid, boil, without stirring, until mixture reaches 155°C when tested with a sweets thermometer or until mixture reaches hard crack stage. Remove from heat, stir in butter. Pour into greased 23cm square cake pan. Mark butterscotch into squares when almost set. Break into squares when cold, wrap in cellophane; store in a cool, dry place.
    Makes about 60.

Pistachio Turkish Delight

2 cups sugar
3 cups water
¼ teaspoon tartaric acid
¾ cup cornflour
1¾ cups icing sugar mixture
1 teaspoon rosewater
2 drops pink food colouring
½ cup shelled pistachios
½ cup cornflour, extra
½ cup icing sugar, extra

Combine sugar and ½ cup water in saucepan, stir over low heat until sugar is dissolved. Bring to the boil, reduce heat until syrup reaches 115°C when tested with a sweets thermometer or until syrup forms a soft ball when tested in a cup of cold water. Add tartaric acid, remove from heat.

Combine cornflour and sifted icing sugar in a bowl, add ½ cup water, stir until smooth. Bring remaining water to the boil in small saucepan, whisk into the cornflour mixture. Return mixture to saucepan, stir over medium heat until mixture boils and thickens. Add syrup gradually, stirring constantly over heat. Continue to boil gently for 30 minutes, without stirring. Add rosewater, food colouring and pistachios. Pour mixture into greased 20cm square pan. Stand for several hours until set. Cut into squares using a wet knife. Toss squares in combined sifted cornflour and icing sugar. Store in airtight container.

Makes about 20.

Mocha Fudge

500g dark chocolate, broken into
   pieces
400g can sweetened condensed milk
60g butter
1 tablespoon instant coffee
1 teaspoon boiling water

Grease and line lamington pan with foil. Place chocolate, condensed milk and butter in saucepan, stir constantly over low heat until mixture is smooth. Blend coffee and water together until coffee is dissolved, add to chocolate mixture, stir until evenly combined. Pour into prepared pan, refrigerate until set. Cut into squares to serve.

Cover with plastic wrap and refrigerate until required.

Makes about 30.

LEFT: Pistachio Turkish Delight.
ABOVE: Mocha Fudge.

Peanut Brittle

1 cup water
2 cups sugar
1 cup light corn syrup
2 cups shelled raw peanuts
30g butter
¼ teaspoon bicarbonate of soda

Place water in saucepan, bring to the boil. Remove from heat, stir in sugar until dissolved. Add corn syrup and peanuts, return to medium heat, cook until mixture reaches 146°C when tested with a sweets thermometer or until mixture reaches hard crack stage. Stir mixture occasionally to keep peanuts submerged. Remove from heat, stir in butter and bicarbonate of soda. Pour into well greased lamington pan. Break into pieces when cool; store in airtight container.

Makes about 1 kilogram.

Honey Nougat

1 cup hazelnuts
1 cup sugar
½ cup water
¾ cup honey
1 egg white

Toast hazelnuts in moderate oven on oven tray for 10 minutes. While nuts are warm, rub off skins using a clean tea-towel.

Place sugar and water in small saucepan, stir over low heat until sugar is dissolved. Cook syrup, without stirring, until it reaches 140°C when tested with a sweets thermometer or until syrup reaches soft crack stage. Stir honey into syrup and return to the boil until temperature is 140°C when tested with a sweets thermometer or until syrup reaches soft crack stage. Beat egg white until stiff peaks form, continue to beat egg white while adding the hot syrup in a thin stream. Beat mixture constantly until it thickens and becomes stiff. Fold through hazelnuts, pour into lightly greased 18cm square pan. Allow to cool and set overnight. Cut into bars using a wet knife. Wrap each piece of nougat in cellophane; refrigerate until required.

Makes about 20.

BELOW: Peanut Brittle.
RIGHT: Honey Nougat.

Photography: Andre Martin
Styling: Michelle Gorry

FOOD FANCIES

From our quaint mini plum puddings and flowerpot-baked bread through to our elegant liqueur fruits and scrumptiously chunky preserves you'll find it hard to decide just what to make. To dress up your homemade gift add a touch of trailing ribbon and an inspired message. Many of these foods can be kept for long periods of time if stored correctly.

Strawberries in Rum

1 cup sugar
½ cup water
2 x 250g punnets strawberries, washed, hulled
½ cup white rum

Place sugar and water in saucepan. Bring to the boil, stirring constantly. Cook, without stirring, until temperature reaches 110°C when tested with a sweets thermometer or until mixture becomes a thin, clear syrup; syrup should not colour.

Pack prepared strawberries into warm, sterilised jars. Stir rum into sugar syrup, pour syrup over strawberries, seal. Store in refrigerator until required.

Pineapple in Malibu

1 cup sugar
½ cup water
1 pineapple, peeled, cored, sliced
½ cup Malibu

Combine sugar and water in saucepan. Bring to the boil, stirring constantly. Cook, without stirring, until temperature reaches 110°C when tested with a sweets thermometer or until mixture becomes a thin, clear syrup; syrup should not colour.

Pack prepared pineapple into warm, sterilised jars. Stir Malibu into sugar syrup, pour over pineapple, seal. Store in refrigerator until required.

Peaches in Grand Marnier

1 cup sugar
½ cup water
6 peaches, peeled, halved
½ cup Grand Marnier

Place sugar and water in saucepan. Bring to the boil, stirring constantly. Cook, without stirring, until temperature reaches 110°C when tested with a sweets thermometer or until mixture becomes a thin, clear syrup; syrup should not colour.

Pack prepared peaches into warm, sterilised jars. Stir Grand Marnier into sugar syrup, pour over peaches, seal. Store in refrigerator until required.

Liqueur Fruits
Any seasonal fruit can be prepared in this way using your favourite liqueur.

LEFT: From left: Peaches in Grand Marnier, Pineapple in Malibu, Strawberries in Rum.

Jars: Accoutrement

Mixed Fruit Jam

Jam will keep for at least 12 months if cooked and sealed properly. Jams reach jelling point around 105°-106°C when tested with a sweets thermometer. If you don't have a sweets thermometer drop a teaspoon of jam onto a freezer-chilled saucer; return it to freezer until jam reaches room temperature. If the jam is ready it should form a skin which wrinkles when pushed with your finger.

2 oranges, finely chopped
1 lemon, finely chopped
2 cups water
6 peaches, peeled, chopped
6 pears, peeled, chopped
2 apples, peeled, chopped
1¼kg sugar

Combine oranges, lemon and water in saucepan. Bring to the boil, boil for 10 minutes. Add peaches, pears, apples and sugar, stir over moderate heat until sugar is dissolved. Bring to the boil, boil, uncovered, for about 1 hour or until jam jells when tested on a chilled saucer; cool slightly. Pour into warm, sterilised jars right to the top, jam will shrink on cooling. Seal when cold, store in a cool, dark place.

Makes about 6 cups.

Sesame Crackers

These crackers will freeze for up to 2 months. Crackers are best served with cheese or dip.
To toast sesame seeds, stir constantly over moderate heat in heavy pan until lightly browned. Their natural oils will be enough to brown them. Cool on kitchen towel or plate.

2 cups plain flour
1½ teaspoons baking powder
1 teaspoon salt
3 tablespoons sesame seeds, toasted
30g butter, melted
¼ cup natural yoghurt
⅔ cup water

Sift flour, baking powder and salt together. Add toasted sesame seeds, butter and yoghurt, mix in enough water to form a stiff dough; knead dough lightly. Roll dough out to 3mm thickness on lightly floured surface, cut into shapes with 5cm round cutter. Prick shapes with fork, place onto lightly greased oven tray. Bake in moderate oven for 10 minutes or until light brown; cool on wire racks. Store crackers in a cool, dry cupboard in an airtight container.

Makes about 25.

LEFT: Mixed Fruit Jam.
BELOW: Sesame Crackers.

Left: Tablecloth, cushions and teddy bears: Belinda's Corner Shop. Basket: Home and Garden

Berry Vinegars

Preparing fruit vinegars is much simpler than most would imagine. We made raspberry, blueberry and strawberry vinegars.

500g fresh berries (raspberries, blueberries or strawberries, hulled), washed
2 cups white wine vinegar

Wash berries and place in sterilised glass jar with tight fitting lid. Pour vinegar over berries, seal, shake and stand on a sunny window sill for 3 weeks, shaking each day. Top with extra vinegar as required. Strain into bowl through colander lined with muslin or a clean tea-towel. Leave to drip for several hours, discard fruit. Bottle vinegar in warm, sterilised bottles, seal. Store in a cool, dark cupboard.
Makes about 2 cups.

Champagne Mustard

1 cup white mustard seeds
2 cups champagne vinegar

Place mustard seeds in a glass jar. Warm vinegar gently in small saucepan, pour over mustard seeds, seal; stand in a cool, dark place. Allow to steep for 2 weeks. Blend mustard in a food processor until smooth, or pound using a mortar and pestle, sieve mustard. Pour into sterilised jars, seal; refrigerate until required.
Makes about 1½ cups.

LEFT: Berry Vinegars.
BELOW: Champagne Mustard.

Left: Bottles: Accoutrement. Below: Cloth: Les Olivades. Box: Home and Garden. Basket and dish: Balmain Linen and Lace

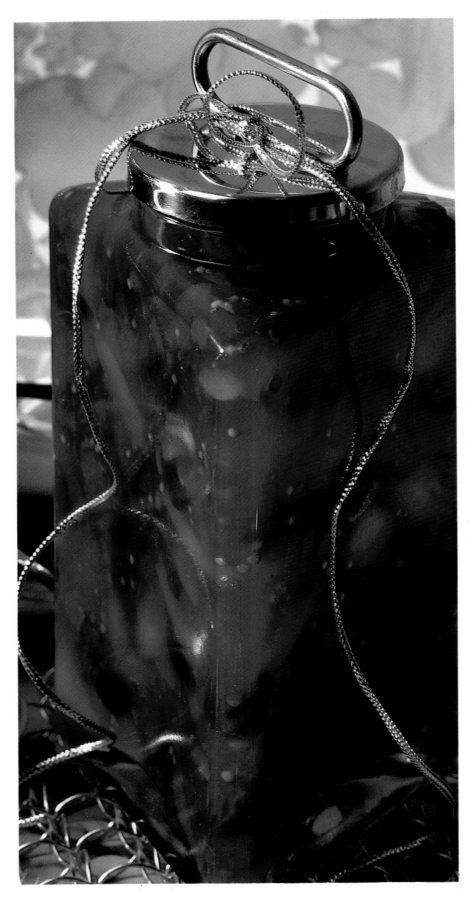

Apricot Chutney

2½ cups brown sugar
2 cups white vinegar
2kg apricots, pitted, chopped
3 onions, chopped
250g sultanas
1 cinnamon stick
2 teaspoons mustard seeds
2 teaspoons ground cloves
1 teaspoon pepper

Place sugar and vinegar in saucepan, stir over moderate heat until sugar is dissolved. Add apricots, onions, sultanas and spices. Bring to the boil, reduce heat, cook for 45 minutes or until mixture thickens; cool slightly. Pour into warm, sterilised jars, seal. Refrigerate until required.

Makes about 3 cups.

Pickled Capsicum

14 capsicum, assorted colours, cored,
   seeded
24 small pickling onions, peeled
2 cups cider vinegar
1 cup sugar
1 tablespoon salt
2 teaspoons white mustard seeds
5 bay leaves
1 tablespoon black peppercorns
5 small red chillies

Chop capsicum into about 2cm squares. Cover capsicum and onions with boiling water in a bowl, stand for 1 minute; drain. Place mixture in large saucepan, cover with cold water. Bring to the boil, drain. Combine vinegar, sugar, salt, mustard seeds, bay leaves, peppercorns and chillies in saucepan, bring to the boil. Add capsicum and onions, simmer for 10 minutes. Spoon mixture into warm, sterilised jars, seal.

Makes about 5 cups.

LEFT: Apricot Chutney.
ABOVE RIGHT: Pickled Capsicum.
RIGHT: Tomato Sauce.

Tomato Sauce

3 tablespoons olive oil
1 onion, chopped
3 cloves garlic, crushed
1 carrot, chopped
1 stick celery, chopped
1 teaspoon chopped fresh oregano
1 teaspoon chopped fresh parsley
1kg tomatoes, chopped
1 teaspoon black peppercorns
1 tablespoon white wine vinegar
1 teaspoon sugar
1 bay leaf
½ cup water

Heat oil in large saucepan. Add onion, garlic, carrot, celery, oregano and parsley; cook until soft. Add tomatoes, peppercorns, vinegar, sugar, bay leaf and water; simmer, uncovered, for 30 minutes. Remove bay leaf and discard, puree mixture in food processor until smooth. Press through a sieve; cool slightly. Pour into warm, sterilised bottles, seal. Sauce is best refrigerated until required.

Makes about 2 cups.

Shortbread

Shortbread will keep in an airtight container for about 2 weeks. It can also be frozen successfully for up to 4 months.

250g butter
½ cup castor sugar
4 cups plain flour

Cream butter and sugar in small bowl with electric mixer until light and fluffy. Stir in sifted flour, knead for 10 minutes. Roll dough out to 1cm thickness on lightly floured surface, cut into 7cm rounds using fluted cutter. Place on lightly greased oven trays, bake in slow oven for 30 minutes; cool shortbread on wire rack.

Makes about 15.

Mini Plum Puddings

¼ cup brandy
¼ cup sultanas
¼ cup raisins, chopped
¼ cup currants
⅓ mixed glace cherries, chopped
¼ cup chopped glace apricots
90g butter
¼ cup brown sugar
⅓ cup chopped blanched almonds
250g plain sweet biscuits, crushed

ROYAL ICING
1 egg white
2 cups pure icing sugar, sifted
½ teaspoon lemon juice

Warm brandy gently. Combine prepared fruit and brandy in bowl; cover, refrigerate for 2 days. Melt butter and sugar in saucepan on moderate heat until sugar is dissolved. Add to fruit mixture with almonds and biscuit crumbs; mix to combine. Roll tablespoons of mixture into balls, place on foil-covered trays. Refrigerate until set, decorate with royal icing.

Royal Icing: Place egg white in bowl, beat lightly until foamy. Add icing sugar 1 tablespoon at a time, beating continuously until mixture forms stiff peaks. Blend in lemon juice. Keep icing covered with plastic wrap until it is required, as it will harden quickly.

Makes about 25.

BELOW: Shortbread.
RIGHT: Mini Plum Puddings.
BELOW RIGHT: Sweet Berry Sauce.

Below: Tablecloth and tray: Home and Garden.Right: Tray: Country Form. Below right: Bottle: Flossoms

Sweet Berry Sauce

1 cup water
2 cups sugar
250g punnet strawberries, washed, hulled
200g punnet raspberries, washed
425g can blueberries, drained
425g can boysenberries, drained
1 teaspoon grated lemon rind

Combine water and sugar in saucepan over low heat, stir until sugar is dissolved. Bring to the boil, reduce heat, simmer for 10 minutes. Slice strawberries thinly, combine with syrup. Add raspberries, blueberries, boysenberries and lemon rind; simmer for 5 minutes or until berries are soft; cool slightly. Pour into warm, sterilised bottles, seal. Refrigerate until required.

Makes about 4 cups.

Green Peppercorn Pate

500g chicken livers
50g butter
1 onion, chopped
1 clove garlic, crushed
55g can green peppercorns, drained
⅓ cup brandy
⅓ cup cream
½ teaspoon ground sage
½ teaspoon ground thyme
100g butter, extra

Wash and trim livers, slice in half. Heat butter in skillet, add onions and garlic, cook until soft. Add green peppercorns and livers, cook until livers are pink (about 4 minutes), add brandy, warm through. Place liver mixture into food processor, process until smooth, add cream, sage and thyme, process until combined. Pour mixture into 2 x 2 cup pate dishes. Melt extra butter, spoon onto top of pate to seal. Refrigerate until required.

BELOW: Green Peppercorn Pate.
RIGHT: Five Grain Bread with
Avocado Butter.
Below: Pate dish: Accoutrement
Photography: Andre Martin
Styling: Michelle Gorry

Five Grain Bread

An easy way to test if bread is cooked properly is to tap the top and bottom of the loaf – it should give a hollow sound at both ends if ready.

2 tablespoons active dry yeast
⅓ cup lukewarm water
½ teaspoon sugar
1 cup water, extra
½ cup cracked wheat
60g butter
2 tablespoons honey
2 tablespoons malt
½ cup milk
½ cup cooked rice
½ cup fine oatmeal
½ cup rye flour
1 cup wholemeal plain flour
4 cups plain flour
2 tablespoons milk, extra

Dissolve yeast in lukewarm water with sugar, allow to stand in warm place until frothy. Place extra water and cracked wheat in small saucepan, cook over medium heat until water has been absorbed and mixture is thick. Remove from heat, stir in butter, honey, malt, milk and rice, allow mixture to cool. Combine flours and oatmeal in large bowl, stir in wheat and yeast mixture, mix to form a dough. Knead mixture on floured surface for about 10 minutes, or until dough springs back when lightly touched with fingers.

Cut dough into 3 pieces for large pots, 4 for medium pots or 8 for small pots. Knead pieces into rounds, place into clean terracotta flower pots. Stand in a warm place for 15 minutes or until doubled in bulk. Glaze with extra milk, bake in moderate oven 35 minutes for large pots, 20 minutes for medium pots or 15 minutes for small pots or until cooked when tested.

Avocado Butter

1 ripe avocado
75g butter
1 tablespoon lemon juice
few drops Tabasco sauce
freshly ground black pepper

Slice avocado in half, remove stone and skin. Place avocado, butter, juice and sauce in a food processor, process until mixture is smooth. Season with black pepper, press into shells or moulds; freeze until required.

Makes about ½ cup.

PACKAGED TO SUIT

Imagine receiving a birthday or Christmas present bursting with goodies which reflect your whims or fancies, personality or passions, favourite colours or hobbies. A 'theme' gift offers the flagging or frustrated gift giver in all of us a way to put energy, fun and the personal touch back into gift giving. So put aside those faithful stand-bys such as perfume, wine, books, chocolates, tools, music and flowers and put your imagination to work! Judy Hubbard explains how easily it can be done.

Put yourself in the other person's shoes – what would really tickle their fancy, not yours? What would they really enjoy receiving, not what would you like giving! The beauty of a theme gift is that the possibilities are endless, and it's unlikely you'll ever give or receive two theme gifts that are exactly the same! These gifts are originals! So, what can you give an ace gardener, a fisherman or triathelete, or a 15-year-old godchild living on another planet to you? Here's a few quick suggestions.

A Fanatical Fisherman

Include a bag full of alluring professional tackle – hooks, lines and sinkers, a magazine, book about knots, lures, perhaps even a fish smoker – all bought from a specialist fishing shop. For fun, add a tin of sardines and a picture or cut-out of the one that got away!

A Teenage Godchild

A Sun Worshipper's Survival pack is just the thing. Fill a sarong or carry bag with a handful of these: flouro zinc pots, creams, visors, insect repellent, a bottle of weak tea (for sunburn!), wine cask "pillow", handwritten tanning hints, an eggtimer to prevent burning, mats, a beach towel, magazines, tissues, spending money, fruit boxes or shades. Cool!

A Super Fit Triathlete

You can't go past the sporty necessities like goggles, bandages, Dencorub, sweat bands, vitamins and health foods, snazzy leotard or running shoes, a magazine and pin-up photo of the stars, bundled into a snappy sports bag.

A Dedicated Gardener

Gather a selection of gourmet gardening gear – smart trowels, pretty gloves, handcream, secateurs, bulbs, seedlings, potting mix, gardening book or diary, plus any whimsical accessories you can find. A green frog, garden gnome or packet of bandaids could be fun. Present them popping out of the pocket of a practical gardening apron, caught under the band of a new straw gardening hat, or peeping from a big plastic bucket decked with a giant crepe bow.

It's Teatime

Whether their passion is Earl Grey, herbal orange zinger, or classic chamomile, tea connoisseurs of any age will enjoy a parcel of elegant teatime accessories to enhance the tea making ritual. This is a super gift for elderly relatives who say they don't need anything. They always need a cuppa!

RIGHT: It's Teatime.

China: Mikasa Tableware. Napkin: Balmain Linen and Lace

CONTENTS
Exotic flavoured teas and bags, strainer, bone china teacup or mug, shortbread biscuits, cotton napkins, shaped or simple sugar cubes in a cellophane bag with ribbon.

INEXPENSIVE EXTRAS
Lemon and lemon press, handwritten scroll – "How to make the perfect cup of tea", homemade almond tuiles or brandy snaps, pastel paper napkins, posy of flowers or bunch of lavender,

fresh scones and jam pots for a portable Devonshire tea, Victoria sandwich, teacake or sacher torte, lamingtons, anzac biscuits or butterfly cakes.

CREME DE LA CREME
Antique tea caddy, book on reading tealeaves, pretty side plates, sugar bowl and creamer, silver tray, spoons, strainer, eccentric teapot, thermos, miniature tea service, cosy tea-cosy, damask napkins.

PRESENTATION IDEAS
* A wicker basket lined with cottage-style fabric, with a pretty gift tag.
* Arrange items on an inexpensive plastic tray, wrap in cellophane dotted with silver stars.
* Fill a box with shredded cellophane, bury tissue wrapped treasures, cover. Add a giant cutout teapot or "T" on top.
* Fill a plain wooden box with straw.
* For a comic touch, a quaint op shop handbag filled with goodies, and labelled "Tea Bag"!

We have listed a variety of items for each pack, but don't feel you have to include each one! Select a few things and package them thoughtfully. If you need inspiration check the A-Z of ideas at the end of this chapter for more ideas.

Adorable Teddies

No-one is too old for a huggable teddy or two. Make up a huddle of cute bears and accessories, and wait for the sighs of delight.

CONTENTS
Tiny teddy bears in any shape, colour or texture, teddy bears' picnic goods – tablecloth, cups, Tiny Teddy biscuits, honey sandwiches, teddy bear stamps and stickers, motifs, pictures, colouring books, a Paddington bear book, teddy bear soaps.

INEXPENSIVE EXTRAS
Decorated homemade teddy bear biscuits, clothes and bows for bare bears, like tulle tutus, gathered onto a ribbon band, the words to the song "The Teddy Bears' Picnic", witty bear tag – prettiest bear, cuddliest bear, best dressed bear, personality bear, set of bear-sized homemade pillows or blankets, packet of jelly bears.

CREME DE LA CREME
Giant teddy, with satin bow, teddy bear china, a teddy cake iced in brown with a pink paper hat and ribbon bow tie.

PRESENTATION IDEAS
* Bundle in pretty floral, gingham, calico or lace, and present in a pastel-painted cane basket.
* Make a bed to display the bears, using a covered shoe box and dainty paper.
* With four bears, pop into a pair of pretty socks, then tie together with a wide satin bow.
* Make a set of drawstring bags, or felt pouches. Write whimsical names in fabric marker on each – Bertie, Basil, Beatrice and Bunny.
* Create a Goldilocks scenario with father bear sporting a bow tie, mother bear a lace apron, and baby bear a big satin bow on its forehead. Add three bowls and spoons and a sign saying "Waiting for Goldilocks".
* Sit teddies in a vine wreath and wrap in cellophane.

LEFT: Adorable Teddies.
ABOVE RIGHT: A Gourmet's Feast.

Left: Basket: Barbara's House and Garden. Teddies: Teddy and Friends the Bear Essentials. Above Right: Terracotta pot: Motyaj Importers

A Gourmet's Feast

A delicious assortment of epicurean delights plus the tools of the trade, is the stuff chefs and gourmets the world over dream about. Also great for difficult people.

CONTENTS
Mouth-watering gourmet foods (cheese, chocolate, herbs, flavoured vinegars and mustards, mayonnaise, marmalades, jellies, jams, sauces, exotic spices, bouquet garni, olive oils), books on unusual cuisines, cooking gadgets – strawberry hullers, mini-whisks, moulds, smart wine or jar labels, bundles of cinnamon sticks, wooden spoons and biscuit cutters, blue and white striped tea-towel.

INEXPENSIVE EXTRAS
Napkins, homemade chocolates or florentines, handwritten favourite recipes.

CREME DE LA CREME
Fresh cream truffles (or better still, real French truffles), wine, wine waiters knives, lace-trimmed napkins and matching rings, champagne pliers, subscription to a food or wine magazine, fresh oysters, nutcracker.

PRESENTATION IDEAS
* Old-fashioned woven hampers always look elegant.
* Slick black paper with real tartan ribbon sets food off to perfection.
* If a basket or a hamper blows the budget, try a cane platter, a covered cardboard box, beribboned hatbox or a large terracotta pot.
* Sash every item with satin ribbon and lace ties or brown parcel labels with witty sayings.
* Use straw, fresh greenery, seed pods and dried pine cones as padding.
* For a mini-version, use a cake tin as the "hamper".

The Gentle Art of Sleeping In

A gift to make those hours lazing in bed even more delicious. With some simple changes in presentation, this parcel could easily become a stylish "Sunday in Bed" or "Breakfast in Bed" kit.

CONTENTS
Books, magazines, newspapers – local and overseas, hot-water bottle and cover, toffees, peppermints or chocolates, blackout mask.

INEXPENSIVE EXTRAS
Earplugs, bed socks, posy of violets or fresh herbs, bookmark, facemask.

CREME DE LA CREME
New nightie, nightshirt, or boxer shorts, breakfast in bed set, smoked salmon, croissants, champagne, relaxing music cassette, personalised china cup and/or tray, classy dressing-gown, luxury toiletries.

PRESENTATION IDEAS
* Use a crisp new pillowcase or stylish black tray for these sleep-in treats.

Personal Party Pack

This parcel of goodies makes a fun gift for a 40th or 50th birthday. Take the contents of a child's take home treat bag and add some fun extras to match age and interests. All the fun of a party without actually having one!

CONTENTS
Blowers, whistle, balloons, sweets, cupcakes, trinkets, dice, tiny books, stickers, funny laces, crayons, bath cubes, toothbrushes, seeds, fridge magnets plastic noses, marbles.

INEXPENSIVE EXTRAS
Life-like finger puppets, handwritten joke cards or fortunes, mock awards for bravery/outstanding performances, miniature personalised cakes, gingerbread hearts or biscuits, a bunch of bright bobbing balloons.

CREME DE LA CREME
Decorative pads, paper, unusual pens and pencils, perfumed soaps.

PRESENTATION IDEAS
* A small cake box, crate or cardboard basket filled with tissue paper, sprinkled with treats.
* A Postpak ready to send and available at any post office.
* Large cellophane bag featuring stickers, a name tag and 6 strands of different coloured curling ribbon.
* Use shoe-laces, real ribbons, hair ties, or lace to tie the parcel.
* Let the whole family share in the celebrations! Make a set of treats bags for everyone in the birthday family.

BELOW: The Gentle Art of Sleeping In.
RIGHT: Personal Party Pack.

Below: China: Mikasa Tableware. Tray, hot-water bottle, cutlery, bookmark: Made Where. Linen: Derek Scott. Bed socks: Foxy Sox. Toiletries: The Body Shop

Simply Cheese and Biscuits

Inspire cheese lovers with some new and unexpected cheeses! A great idea for men who are hard to buy for.

CONTENTS
Platter, cheese (stilton, brie, blue vein, camembert, cheddar), cheese-wire, paper platters and napkins, crusty farmhouse loaf, bottle of tokay, dry biscuits, olives, dates and nuts.

INEXPENSIVE EXTRAS
Fresh herbs, selection of fresh fruits like grapes, strawberries, hand polished apples, or exotics like fresh mangoes, lychees or nashi pears.

CREME DE LA CREME
Wooden bric-a-brac, wooden cheese board, pate knife, a Swedish cheese knife, a superb red wine.

PRESENTATION IDEAS
* Wrap in red check cotton swag, basket or practical storage box.
* For smart portable treats, pack for picnics, the races or watching the cricket, just add a basket or bag with napkins, and two wine glasses.

Presentation Tips
Spend some extra time and care to wrap your collection. Make your intentions clear with lots of fun labels and explanatory notes that show how much time and imagination has been invested. Simply use the list below to mix and match items to suit your theme and budget.

* *An upturned cane sun hat or floppy fabric gardening, bowls or cricket hat (these make perfect small food "hampers" because they fill quickly and look impressive when wrapped).*
* *Shirt box, covered or painted.*
* *Baskets.*
* *Plastic picnic plates or trays.*
* *Colourful crates.*
* *Tea-towels or napkins.*
* *Cottage print fabrics or calico.*
* *Big terracotta flowerpots and planters.*
* *Plastic buckets, or beach buckets.*
* *Painted tins.*
* *Drawstring bags.*
* *Cardboard document folders.*
* *Large socks.*
* *Recyclable shopping bags.*
* *Glass or plastic salad bowls.*
* *Lunch, cake or hat boxes.*
* *Old suitcases, boxes, bags, tubs, and trunks from op-shops or markets.*
* *Straw bags.*
* *Raffia placemats.*
* *A backpack.*

Ageing Gracefully Kit

A package of pure nonsense, ideal for anyone over 40 who can still laugh at themselves and the world!

CONTENTS
Bottle of hair restorer, risque magazine, anti-wrinkle cream, a mug (there are lots of funny ones available on the market) and incontinence pads, magnifying glass, book of crossword puzzles, a diary, worry beads, packet of indigestion tablets.

INEXPENSIVE EXTRAS
Mock meals-on-wheels form, op-shop spectacles with thick frames.

CREME DE LA CREME
A hammock "for naps", a fan or umbrella "for the heat", and a bird feeder or wind chimes "for reflecting".

PRESENTATION IDEAS
* Stack into a useful straw bag.
* Wrap in thermal underwear!

LEFT: Simply Cheese and Biscuits.
ABOVE: Ageing Gracefully Kit.
Left: Basket: Barbara's House and Garden. Cheese board: Opus. Above: Diary: Opus. Men's toiletries: The Body Shop.

Hassled Parents' Hamper

Calm the jagged nerves and restore a lost sense of humour with this practical parents' panacea!

CONTENTS
Bottles of vitamins, escapist magazines, breakfast in bed voucher, cooling eye mask, bunch of flowers, champagne, earplugs, gentle music tape, aspirin, bandaids, Life Savers, 6 dummies or a bottle of gripe water, smelling salts, perfumed sachets.

INEXPENSIVE EXTRAS
Voucher for baby-sitting, homemade dinner for two or weekend without the children voucher, homemade cake or delicious casserole.

PRESENTATION IDEAS
* Pile into a recyclable shopping bag sporting a tag reading "We understand" or "Things *will* get better".

LEFT: A Winter's Tale.
BELOW: Hassled Parents' Hamper.
RIGHT: Letter Boxes.

Left: Basket: Barbara's House and Garden. Socks, scarf: Foxy Sox. Massage Oil: The Body Shop. Hot-water bottle: Made Where. Below: Eye Mask: The Body Shop. Right: Wine basket: Balmain Linen and Lace. Pen, paperweight, mug, pencils and pencil holder, paperknife: Made Where

A Winter's Tale

Just the thing for rainy, wintry birthdays! Add a relaxing book, cushion, and some worry beads to create a comfort kit for anyone who'd enjoy the cosy feeling of sinking into a big soft chair in front of a log fire.

CONTENTS
Interesting mug, packet of pea soup, small bottle of brandy, handwritten recipe for glogg (see below) or gluwein and a bundle of ingredients, warm, inviting hiking socks, hot-water bottle, tartan foot rug, massage body oil to go with massage book, cough drops.
Swedish Glogg : Mix lemon slices, ½ teaspoon whole cloves, 4 strips orange peel, 2 cinnamon sticks, ½ cup sugar, and a cup raisins and whole almonds in bowl. Steep in a bottle of dry red wine for 6 hours. Strain, warm up, and glogg, glogg, glogg, as the Swedes' say!

INEXPENSIVE EXTRAS
Bundle of vitamin C tablets, jar of homemade oatmeal biscuits or bran muffins, packet of hot chocolate, lemons and a pot of honey, homemade fudge, flu tablets.

CREME DE LA CREME
Rustic handknitted jumper or leg warmers, tapestry kit, angora scarf, Irish coffee mugs or glasses, leather gloves, felt hat, bottle of very old, smooth Scotch whisky or tawny port, deep and meaningful book, 5,000 piece jigsaw puzzle, argyle socks, book on massage, cuddly toy.

PRESENTATION IDEAS
* This parcel needs to feel warm, so wrap everything in soft fabrics then bundle into a basket or flannelette pillowcase. If the gift giving occasion falls near the winter solstice on June 22, give your wrapping an upside-down Christmas flavour.

Letter Boxes

Useful yet personal, this versatile theme gift will be well used by a young girl or boy, a retired octogenarian or anyone in between. Just choose colours and paper motifs that match their personal style.

CONTENTS
Loose sheets of coloured paper/notelets, envelopes, stamps, aerograms, mug, colourful paperclips, notebook or address book, wax and seal, plain visiting cards, blank picture cards.

INEXPENSIVE EXTRAS
Rubbers, pencils, stickers and stars.

CREME DE LA CREME
Roll of printed names and addresses, gold and silver pens, printed and personalised notepapers, perfumed papers, book about letter writing, making marbled paper, or calligraphy, birthday book, letter opener, paperweight, pencil tray, letter rack, leather desk set.

PRESENTATION IDEAS
* Buy a decorative papier-mache box.
* Decorate and personalise a manila document folder with stickers, ribbons and a name.

Lovable Eccentrics' Pack

Be adventurous with this collection of small gifts that reflect someone's personality, ideas and personal style. An exuberant, larger-than-life friend might inspire a collection like:

CONTENTS
Bright red nail polish, shimmering scarf, oversized key ring, flashy vase, 500 grams of pink jelly beans, bow tie in spots, paisley or garish geometrics.

INEXPENSIVE EXTRAS
Fake jewels, glitzy op-shop earrings, gold chocolate coins, large block of rich chocolate.

CREME DE LA CREME
Showy perfume bottle, handpainted terracotta pots, plaque or platter.

PRESENTATION IDEAS
* A reusable Lurex wrap is ideal or an off-beat op-shop hat.
* A shiny box filled with pink jelly beans and gold coins.

You-Can-Do-It Kit!

Help someone discover a new craft or hobby with a collection of basic starter equipment for wood carving, upholstery, quilting, folk art, naive painting, decoupage, picture framing, cross-stitch, or china painting. See The Australian Women's Weekly Home Library's *Decorative Crafts* or *Fete Favourites* for ideas.

CONTENTS
Craft materials, glue, lacquer paint pots, brushes, craft kit.

INEXPENSIVE EXTRAS
Packet of bandaids, headache tablets or worry beads, magazine, handwritten award for Novice Quilter of the Year.

PRESENTATION IDEAS
* Use sacks, pillowcases, baskets and buckets, or simply wrap items in bright glossy paper with a bold sign.
* In a similar vein, a first home owner, flat dweller, teenager, retired hobbyist or Do-It-Yourself novice might enjoy basic handyman requisites – hammer, spanner, screwdriver, chisel, power lock tape measure, putty knife wire brush, scraper-presented in a metal tool box. This is an expensive gift, so only include one or two larger items.
* If the DO-IT pack has big items in it, like a spade, wheelbarrow, or rubbish bin, simply attach a ball of string, conceal the unwieldy gift in a shed, or next door, and present the end of the string, with tag, to the recipient.

How Utterly Romantic

Wear your heart unashamedly on your sleeve with a classic romantic gift package. Perfect for Valentine's day, an engagement, a wedding anniversary or a wedding, a very special birthday, or for a little girl's 5th birthday.

CONTENTS
Heart-shaped soaps, biscuits, chocolates, bunch of violets, forget-me-nots, old photo frame with a nostalgic photo, dated and named in gold letraset on the mount, a framed baby or childhood picture, lace hanky or garter, silky lingerie or bed linen, poetry.

ABOVE LEFT: Lovable Eccentrics' Pack.
LEFT: How Utterly Romantic.
ABOVE RIGHT: You-Can-Do-It Kit.

Above left: Jewellery: Tinseltown. Left: Lingerie, lace cushion, frame with baby photo, small box: Balmain Linen and Lace. Perfumed soaps, potpourri, garter, bath perfumes, handkerchief: Time Was. Silver frame: Whitehill Silver and Plate Co. Hat box: Janet Niven Antiques. Above right: Craft items: Stadia Handcrafts.

INEXPENSIVE EXTRAS
Handwritten scroll with red velvet tie, romantic verses – copied or straight from the heart (romantic rhyming words like love, dove, croon, tune, moon might help you get started), homemade card with white lace edging, a buttonhole, fresh from the garden, pictures and cards showing love birds, cupids and arrows, roses and hearts, heart-shaped cake, homemade heart-shaped gingerbread biscuits, homemade Victorian style card with lacy doily cut-outs and evocative, silvery writing.

CREME DE LA CREME
Diamonds, pearls or any other precious stone, perfume romantic novel, silver picture frame engraved with dates and names, straw hat with satin bow, lace collar, satin bed linen, tuberoses, frangipani, freesias, or any other fragrant flowers, champagne and two crystal flutes, loving cup, gold or silver ring, miniature topiary rose bush.

PRESENTATION IDEAS
* Arrange items in a box, nestling each in a flurry of white tissue. Wrap the box in pastel glossy paper and tie with a 2cm wide piece of lace. Tuck a posy of dainty fabric flowers into the bow.
* Scour antique shops for a quaint tin or container that gives a Victorian feel to the gift.
* Decorate a parcel or basket with sprigs of gypsophila, silver stickers and white doves.
* A pretty plate makes a good presentation base.
* White gloss paper looks dramatic with matching card and flowers on top.
* Tie a string of hearts around the gift by concertina folding the required length of red paper and carefully cutting out a heart shape.
* Sprinkle the parcel with potpourri or confetti just before giving.
* Simply garnish the gift with a funny romantic saying written onto the paper like: "Love is like the measles; we all have to go through it" (Jerome Jerome) or Napoleon's memorable "I have seen only you, I have admired only you, I desire only you."

Spectators' Pack

A pack of essentials for any serious sport's spectator!

CONTENTS
Pen on a rope, crossword puzzle, cushion in team colours, pocket dictionary of sport, disposable hat, dictionary of colloquialisms for creative barracking, throat lozenges.

INEXPENSIVE EXTRAS
Ribbons and homemade rosettes in team colours, nibbles.

CREME DE LA CREME
Binoculars.

PRESENTATION IDEAS
* Wrap in an old or new rug, or decorate a box with a favourite team's colours.
* Wrap goodies in the sports pages of your newspaper.

Little Luxuries Pack

Pamper someone special with a parcel of indulgences that has the feel of plush velvet and an aura of luxury, however fleeting. A great gift for unbirthdays when someone just needs cheering up or to feel special.

CONTENTS
Smoked salmon and caviar, rich chocolate truffles, pate de foie gras, tiny toasts to go with pate, petit fours, potpourri, rosewater.

INEXPENSIVE EXTRAS
Fake pearls, tortoiseshell comb, replica car or posh key ring, fun vouchers promising fun fantasies like "A trip around the world for two...on a tandem bicycle!", "A fat cheque for $10 million dollars", "10 year's supply of wonderful Beluga caviar."

CREME DE LA CREME
French champagne, imported chocolates, quartz crystal or thunder egg, silk camisole, handkerchief or bow tie, bath head cushion, kimono, fresh orchids, mud mask, voucher for a facial or massage, quilted evening bag, jewellery, silver tray, sea sponges, perfumed soaps, bath oils and salts, face and body creams, velour towels, red roses, exotic perfumes like Poison or Opium.

PRESENTATION IDEAS
* A basket or shiny card box.
* For a stunning effect, scatter items on pieces of shiny chintz, rich dark leopard fabric, laces, or moire taffeta.
* Tie gift with a silky cord with tassels.
* Present extravagances in a panama hat or a dapper straw boater.
* A large sea-shell.

BELOW: Spectators' Pack.
RIGHT: Little Luxuries Pack.

Photography: Jon Bader

Styling: Marie-Helene Clauzon

QUICK & EASY PACKS

Colour Their World

Collect a range of treats big and small but in only one or two colours. Whether you choose a dramatic black/white, black/pink, pastel pink, midnight blue, a favourite team's colours, a jet black pack, or elegant white for purists, the impact will be sensational. Wrap and add ribbon to match.

Well Read

Include books, bookmarks and book plates, handmade bookmarks, and another more expensive item like a dictionary, Itty Bitty Book Light, book stand, book voucher, decorative book ends, printed and personalised book plates, head cushion, and for fun a real worm in a match box, clearly marked bookworm!

Being Green Kit

An environmentally aware selection of organic vegetables and herbs, state of the art books, herbal medicines, calico shopping bags, unbleached toilet paper, biodegradable products, packets of tree seeds, recycled notepaper and membership to The Wilderness Society.

Redhead's Survival Pack

Strictly for fun loving carrot-tops, a parcel of sunburn cream, Redhead matches, hair colouring, red hat, red jelly beans and a sharp red pencil. Team up with any other red-hot items you can think of and wrap in red, of course! Blondes, brunettes and greys can be handled with similar style.

Cute Cat Pack

Catch a cat fan catnapping with a collection of catty accessories – tea-towels, cards, stationery, china, key rings, and books. Wrap in cat paper and label CAT-astrophe! or CAT-atonic! or just "For one cute cat!" For fun, include a curly cat quiz – how many words can they make starting with Cat?

Dog, fish and horse lovers' packs are just as easy to create.

FOR KIDS

My Letter Pack

This parcel of goodies, all of which start with the first letter of the recipient's name, is good for any age group. A "P" pack for 6-year-old Peter or Polly, looks something like this list.

CONTENTS
Pen, plane, pencil, plasticine, panda, photo, plate, pencil-sharpener, pipe-cleaners, paper, paints, parasols, puppet, poster.

PRESENTATION IDEAS
* Wrap the gifts then add a giant letter "P" on the outside.
* Present lucky dip style in a bright check bag, marking each item with a big, bright "P".
* Use double-sided adhesive tape to stick wrapped lollies, or bubblegum to the parcel.
* Scroll wrapped gifts in card and wrap as a giant bonbon.

RIGHT: My Letter Pack.

Pencils, paddle-pop sticks, plasticine, paints, paintbrushes, pop-up pen, panda paper: Avalon Toy Shop. White gift box, plate: Ikea. Plane: Coles New World

Music For Your Ears

Watch out Carl Orff, Zoltan Kodaly on Shinichi Suzuki! Here's a pack of musical treats that will really strike a chord with noise loving under 5's. Choose one or two basic items, then add a collection of homemade extras.

CONTENTS
Harmonica, kazoo, recorder, tin drum, tambourine, flutes, xylophones, rattles.

INEXPENSIVE EXTRAS
Homemade shakers, rhythm sticks, whistles and clickers, wooden spoons.

PRESENTATION IDEAS
* Stash in a sturdy crate for easy storage and easy access.

Flighty Fingers and Toes

A real scene stealer for teenage girls! Paraphernalia for keeping fingernails and tootsies in top shape and colour.

CONTENTS
Emery boards, orange sticks, cuticle massage cream, stickers, false nails, different coloured nail enamels, base coat and top coat, pumice stone, nail clippers, foot cream.

INEXPENSIVE EXTRAS
Carton of milk for calcium.

CREME DE LA CREME
Voucher for a professional manicure.

PRESENTATION IDEAS
* Wrap inside a fun pair of knickers or socks, or in a shoulder bag.
* Add some noisy brass bangles and a character hat.

LEFT: Music For Your Ears.
BELOW: Flighty Fingers and Toes.

Left: Music box: Ikea. Tambourine, green flute, cymbals: Avalon Toy Shop. Harmonica: Coles New World. Below: Pencil case, fake nails, nail stickers: Avalon Toy Shop. Socks: Sportsgirl

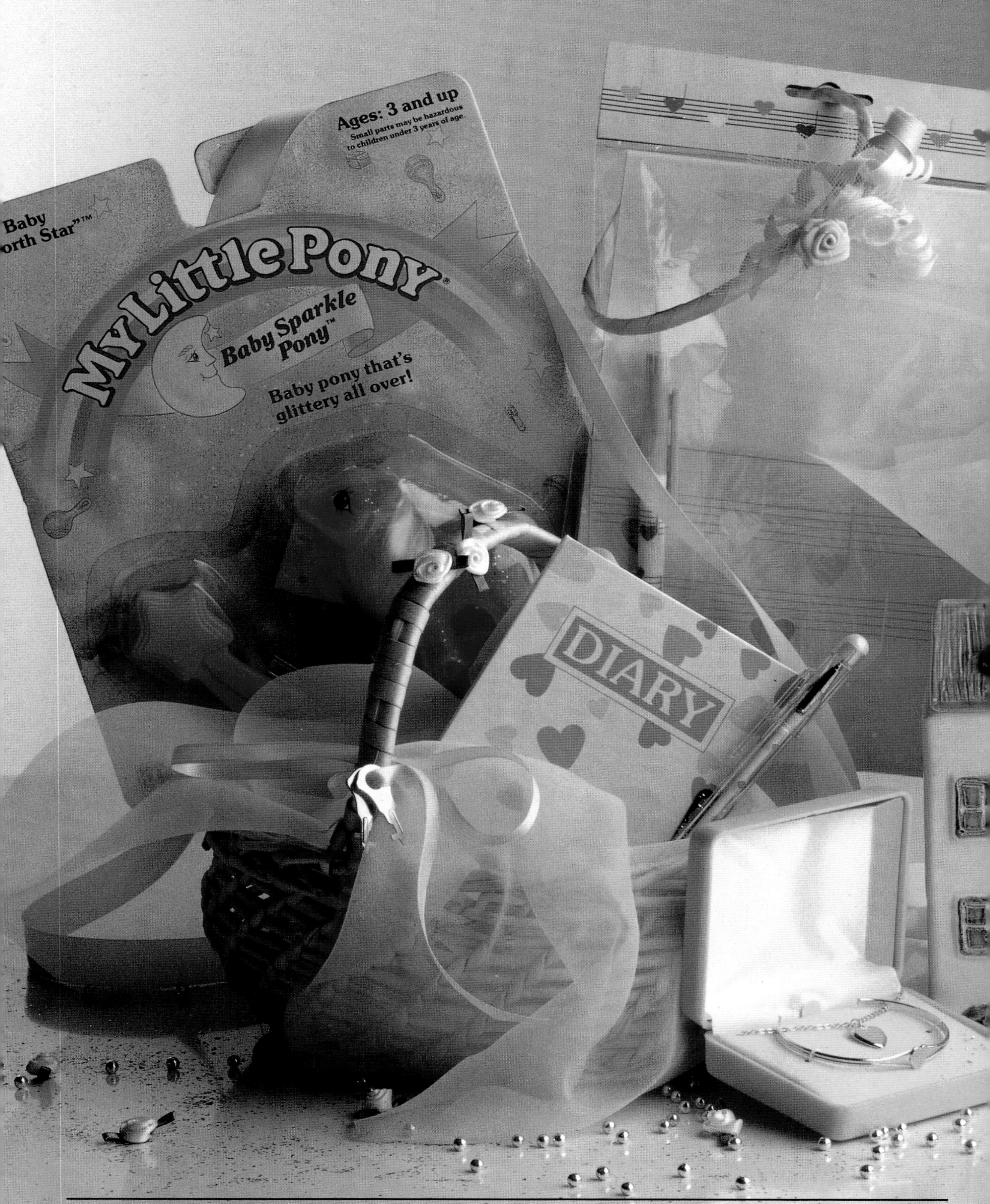
Baby
orth Star"™
Ages: 3 and up
Small parts may be hazardous to children under 3 years of age.
My Little Pony®
Baby Sparkle Pony™
Baby pony that's glittery all over!
DIARY

A Fairy's Child

Suspend belief and re-create the quiet enchanting world of fairies! Design a pretty pink or silver parcel of tiny treasures that will be adored by anyone who still believes.

CONTENTS
A tiny ring, slippers, bell, small soap, fairy dust (glitter), flower fairy book, fairy doll, dreamy necklace, Lilliput size china house.

INEXPENSIVE EXTRAS
Scrolled letter from Queen of the Fairies in wispy silvery writing, sparklers, silver card crown with sequin jewels, fairy wings cut from silver card and sprinkled with glitter, a wand made from dowel with a big silver star and curling ribbon tails, bracelet with a bell attached (so the other fairies can hear you), tiny posy of fresh flowers, plate of tiny meringues, fairy cakes iced in palest pink with silver cachous, a bag of star-shaped biscuits wrapped in a cellophane bag.

PRESENTATION IDEAS
* Paint a basket pink or silver and put in wrapped treasures, delicately labelled in dreamy writing.
* Place each gift in a tiny cane basket.
* Make a fairy wreath by weaving ivy and jasmine around small wire circles.
* Wrap pastel jelly beans or tiny sweets in circles of tulle or lace, and tie with velvet ribbons.
* Cut wide strips of crepe paper, then wrap each item in the paper, winding and adding until a crepe paper ball is made. Mysterious to unravel!
* Wrap gifts in organza or silky satin and dot with rose petals.

LEFT: A Fairy's Child.

Basket, lace, ribbon: Tranquility Base. Costume jewellery, diary, glitter, My Little Pony, hairband, note paper, ball with mini erasers, heart pen: Avalon Toy Shop.

Create-a-Card Kit

Kids adore the glorious mess of glue and glitter that is an essential part of creating a homemade masterpiece.

CONTENTS
Choose from this long list: scissors, felt pens, crayons, craft glue, stapler, stickers, glitter, rolls of coloured card (white, gold, black and silver), individual sheets of paper, fabric flowers, doilies, sequins, alphabet templates, visitor's cards, scraps, ribbons, "eyes" from craft shops, white out, poster paints.

INEXPENSIVE EXTRAS
Old birthday cards, wrapping paper, magazines for cut-outs, shells, dried flowers, cottonwool balls, ribbon bows.

CREME DE LA CREME
Gold and silver pens, calligraphy pen.

PRESENTATION IDEAS
* A covered shoe box, document folder or cellophane bag.

BELOW: Create-a-Card Kit.
RIGHT: Over-the-Rainbow.

Below: Waste-paper basket, Babbla pens: Ikea. Mini briefcase, glue pen, glitter, stamp set, paper mosaics, paper pack, scissors: Avalon Toy Shop. Right: Face paints, balloons, stickers, markers, chalk, note-book, colour packs, book: Avalon Toy Shop. Storage box: Ikea.

Over-the-Rainbow

Under 5's love colour explosions, so the rainbow theme is a natural for them. If you'd prefer, use just one colour for this parcel – like yellow, red, or blue.

CONTENTS
Face paints, crayons, pencils, rubbers, stickers, balloons, packets of smarties, streamers.

INEXPENSIVE EXTRAS
* Make a rainbow shaker by covering a cardboard roll with bright paper, then stick half metre pieces of coloured streamers each end.

PRESENTATION IDEAS
* Bundle each item into a different coloured cotton hanky or felt square.
* Cover the gift with rainbow stickers!

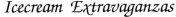

Dashing Pirate Pack

Capture the badness and boldness of pirates and piratesses with a swag of buccaneer goodies.

CONTENTS
Pirate book, gold curtain ring earrings, striped T-shirt, colourful necktie, eye patch, pirate flag, pirate Lego.

INEXPENSIVE EXTRAS
A treasure hunt map with clues, pieces of eight (real coins wrapped in silver foil), rolled newspaper sword or buccaneer's hat.

PRESENTATION IDEAS
* Treasure ahoy! Hollow out a high top loaf, and cut off a lid. Fix licorice straps as metal bands using brass drawing pins. Pile in the treasure!
* Use black paper and paint on white skull and crossbones.
* Make a calico treasure sack and stash gifts inside.

Icecream Extravaganzas

Splendid "spiders" or gorgeous, gooey icecream concoctions, oozing with topping and glistening with sweets, make children, and many adults, melt. Simply give the ingredients needed to be an icecream whizz kid at home!

CONTENTS
Chocolate bits, popcorn, wafer fans, Icemagic, sweets, lemonade, sugar cones, voucher for a tub of icecream!

INEXPENSIVE EXTRAS
Paper napkins, moulds.

CREME DE LA CREME
Parfait glasses and spoons.

PRESENTATION IDEAS
* Decorate a box or crate with a large icecream sign or flag. Yummy!

An A to Z of Inspiration

Anti-flu Kit
Bushman's Kit
Computer Genius Pack
Doll Making Kit
Elderly Gentleman's Pack
Flower Power Pack
Grandmother's Kit
Hospital Survival Pack
Indian Food Connoisseur's Kit
Jellybean-A-Holic's Kit
Letter Writer's Inspiration Parcel
Motivation Kit
Naughty But Nice Kit
Outdoors Kit
Pick-Me-Up Parcel
Quiet Times Bag
Razzle Dazzle Kit
Stress Management Pack
Traveller's Kit
Untidy Person's Kit
Valentine's Day Special
Workaholic's Kit
X-citement Package
Yellow Lover's Kit
Zebra Stripes Pack

BELOW: Dashing Pirate Pack.
RIGHT: Icecream Extravaganzas.

Below: Pirate Lego, dress-up kit, comic book: Avalon Toy Shop. Right: Tray, straws, serviettes, icecream scoop: Ikea. Parfait glasses: The Melbourne Shop

Photography: Tandy Rowley

Styling: Rowena Sheppard

PRESENT APPEAL

You've put time, energy and thought into choosing the perfect gift. Now, for the final touch – the wrapping! Pretty paper and ribbon make an appealing masterpiece, or create a teasing camouflage – whatever the gift don't neglect this part of the presentation.

Economical Wraps

Gifts don't have to be wrapped in expensive gift wrap. A sheet of brown paper, aluminium foil, or newspaper can look exciting with the right trims. Or, bundle your offering in cheap, useful fabric, such as calico – it can be re-used and is no more expensive than gift wrap.

* Wrap a gift in newspaper. Trim it with ribbon, add glitter and stars to create a surprisingly sensational effect.

Concealing Wraps

A concealing wrap is great for those who love to pry, poke and weigh up the gift before it's opened. Here are a few ideas guaranteed to tease the curious.

* Try the old "box within a box within a box" trick, but only if you're sure your recipient can handle the frustration.
* Carefully wrap a tiny gift and position it in a larger box. Hide the gift under a mountain of jelly beans, chocolates, potpourri, or marbles.

BASIC HOW-TO-WRAP
If the gift has an irregular shape, put it in a box; wrapping will be much neater and easier. Cut wrapping paper longer than gift and wide enough to fit around it.

Position gift in centre of paper. Trim paper at each end so excess paper is slightly more than half the gift's depth. Fold paper around gift, turn under overlapping edge, tape in place (use double-sided tape for a neater finish).
Fold in sides of excess paper at each end.

Fold top flap down and bottom flap up, tape in place. Your gift is now perfectly wrapped and ready for trimming.

Creative Additions

Once the paper wrap is complete, add finishing touches with pretty ribbon or fun additions – anything which can be tied around the box is a possibility! Here are some hints and ideas to get you started.

* Wrap your gift in colours to suit the occasion; red and green for Christmas, pastel blue or pink for a new baby, white for a wedding, or match colour of ribbon and paper to gift.
* Tie gift with lengths of cord threaded with tiny toys (see picture below).
* Embellish a plainly wrapped gift with a bunch of fresh or dried flowers (see picture at right).
* Add stickers to a plain paper wrap; animals for pet lovers, cupids for a romantic gift, teddies, etc (see picture at right on opposite page).
* Tie a bunch of balloons on top of your gift for a bright festive feeling (see picture at far right on opposite page).

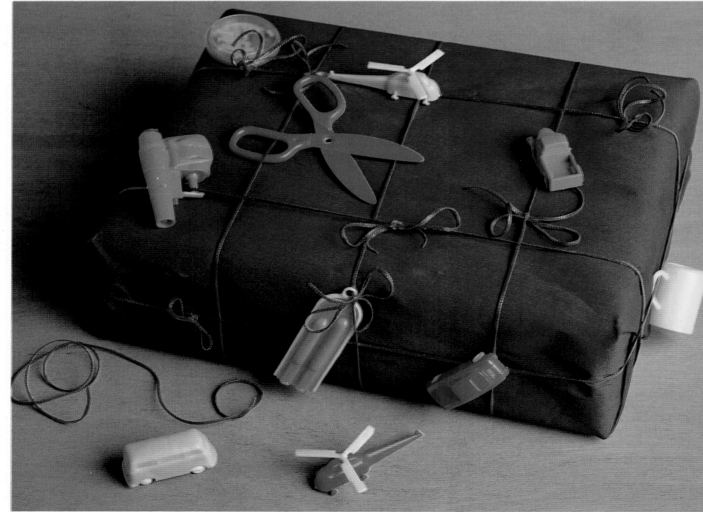

Wrapping Bonus

Choose something out of the ordinary to wrap your gift. This can be related to the occasion, part of the gift, or merely an extra bonus. All you need to add is a ribbon and bow.

Ideas include: nappy to wrap a baby's gift, tea-towel holding kitchen utensils, blanket wrapped around a picnic basket, small tablecloth wrapping a set of cutlery, terracotta pot over-flowing with gardeners' goodies.

* For a delicate effect, choose a lace-edged handkerchief to wrap a tiny gift, tie with ribbon (see picture above).

* Giving a piece of jewellery? Pop it in a box and tie in a pretty silk scarf (see picture at right).

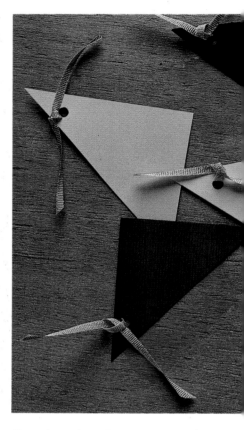

Cards

Cards can be much more than an accompaniment to a gift. Fill a card with confetti, stars or hearts which scatter on opening, or give a handmade card.

Gift Tags

Heavy, coloured paper
Hole-punch
Ribbon

Cut coloured cardboard into geometric shapes. Punch a hole in one corner using a hole-punch. Thread a ribbon through hole.

Embroidered Cards

Presentation frame cards (from craft stores)
Scraps of printed fabric
Six stranded embroidery thread, in colours to match fabric
Glue stick
Lace (optional)
Organza (optional)

Embroider areas of printed fabric you wish to highlight. Use embroidery stitches of your choice and 3 strands of thread in colours to match fabric. See page 124 for stitch instructions.

Trim fabric to fit card. Apply glue to back of card front, around frame area. Position fabric in card with right side facing front.

Lace trim (optional). Cut lace to fit around frame area, glue in place. Glue a ribbon bow at bottom edge of frame, if desired.

Organza overlay (optional). Position organza over fabric, work embroidery through both layers.

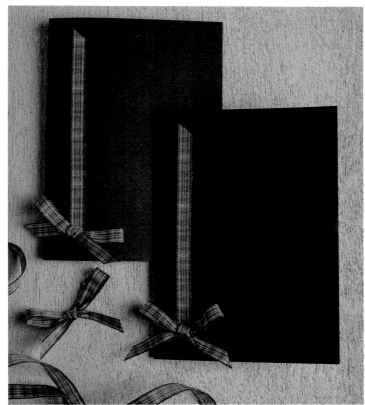

Ribbon-Trimmed Cards

Stationery paper
Ribbon
Glue-stick

Fold sheet of paper in half. Position card to open from right-hand side. Glue length of ribbon to front of card and glue a ribbon bow at one end.

Cross-Stitch Cards

Presentation frame cards (from craft stores)
14-count Aida fabric, to fit card
Six stranded embroidery thread, (see key on page 42 for colours)
Adhesive tape

Work design following instructions for Cross-Stitch Miniatures on page 42 and stitch instructions on page 124.

Position fabric in card frame, right side facing out.

Tape fabric to card.

ABOVE LEFT: Confetti-Filled Card.
LEFT: Embroidered Cards.
ABOVE: Gift Tags.
ABOVE RIGHT: Ribbon-Trimmed Cards.
RIGHT: Cross-Stitch Cards.

Do-It-Yourself Wrapping Paper

Save money and personalise your presents by making your own gift wrap. Simple printing methods can give stunning results and, for the more adventurous, we have detailed steps in the craft of paste-paper making. If you have children, enlist their help; fingerpaintings by tiny tots make wonderful gift wrap.

PRINT-YOUR-OWN GIFT WRAP
Choose sturdy paper for giftwrap; white art paper or brown paper is ideal. Save time by printing several sheets at once; roll them carefully for storage. Experiment with simple printing methods or follow our instructions.
1. Position sections of doilies, leaves, flowers or paper cut-outs on paper. Spray paper with paint, making sure materials don't move. Remove materials and allow paper to dry.

Cut-outs, glitter, stars or confetti can be glued onto the paper for further decoration.
2. Make printing stamps from potato (or sponge). Dip stamp into paint and press onto paper. Crumple a piece of scrap paper and dip into paint. Press on paper.

3. Paint paper with water-thinned paint, allow to dry. Cut out shapes from coloured tissue paper and glue to painted paper.
4. Using white wax-crayon, draw pattern onto absorbent white paper. Paint stripes on paper using water-based paint. The wax-crayon design will resist paint and show through. Splatter paper by running a knife blade across a paint-loaded toothbrush.
5. Brown paper looks fabulous printed with the aid of a drinking straw and water-thinned paint. Dip straw into paint and drop paint onto paper, blow through the straw so paint runs in different directions.
6. Cut-out coloured tissue paper shapes and glue onto paper.
7. Use a small sponge roller, available from hardware stores to paint stripes onto paper. Dip a flat sponge into same colour paint and press lightly onto paper. Repeat until paper is covered.

Paste-Paper

Michael Lester has revived the ancient craft of paste-paper making. He explains some simple but decorative methods which give spectacular results; papers are suitable for gift wrap, book coverings and, in some cases, for framing.

1 cup cornflour
10ml glycerine
20ml liquid detergent
40ml PVA paper glue, flexible drying, acid free (available at art supply stores)
Large sheets of heavy paper
Water-based paints, in desired colours
2 litre plastic bowl
Stainless steel whisk
Large sponge
Spatula
Plastic containers for coloured paste (take-away food containers or margarine containers)
Stocking or pantihose with no holes or runs (for straining paste)
Household utensils to create patterns (we used a palette knife, pressure rollers (available at artist supply stores), fine soft brushes, jar lids and nylon broom head)
Work bench (we used a sheet of acetate tacked to a wooden bench)

Note. It is useful to have a sink handy for frequently washing rollers, brushes and hands. A large space is needed to dry wet paste-paper sheets.

PVA glue is used to prevent cracks in dried paste and to give a water-proof effect to the surface of the paste-paper. **To make paste.** Place cornflour in bowl, gradually add cold water, gently mix with a whisk until it reaches a milky consistency.

Pour approximately 650ml boiling water into mixture while whisking quickly; continue to whisk quickly until mixture becomes translucent.

Add a little cold water to prevent a skin forming on top as paste cools.

When paste is cool, gradually stir in approximately 300ml of cold water until the paste becomes smooth and workable.

Strain paste by spooning it into a stocking using a spatula. Hold stocking at top, run hand down stocking, squeezing paste through the end into a bowl.

Makes about 1 litre.

Preparing paste and adding colours. Add glycerine, detergent and PVA glue to paste, stir until combined. Spoon paste into plastic containers (each container will hold a different colour paste). Add a different paint colour to each container, mix in small amounts gradually until desired colour. The quantity of paint used for each paste colour depends on the type of paint and the depth of colour you desire.

To prepare paper. Cut paper to fit work area, sponge it with water on one side, then the other, smooth out any bubbles or creases. Turn the paper once more, sponge out bubbles and creases again.

To make paste-paper. Spoon a coloured paste onto wet paper, decorate paper with paste as desired.
Decorative techniques. A number of techniques can be used to decorate

OPPOSITE PAGE: Do-It-Yourself Wrapping Paper.
BELOW: Paste-Paper.

paste-paper. Start by trying some of the following ideas, then experiment.

1. Use a pressure roller to spread paste in patterns or to create a background for other patterns. Rollers of different widths are useful.

2. A fine soft brush can be used to spread paste over paper but will soak up paste. Brushes can make swirling patterns which look particularly striking when a brightly coloured paste is used on coloured paper. This technique also makes an attractive background for other patterns.

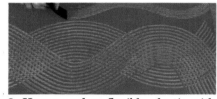

3. Heavy card or flexible plastic with notches cut at regular intervals, or grout scrapers, can be used to comb patterns in paste. Use a brush to apply a thin paste background before combing the pattern.

4. Swirl a plastic paint tray over a paste background to create a "spaghetti" pattern.

5. One of the most effective patterns is made by pulling two paste-loaded papers apart. Use a roller to apply a layer of paste to one sheet of paper, put paper aside. Apply a layer of a second coloured paste to another sheet of paper, then place the first sheet over it. Slowly pull the sheets apart.

A number of different coloured

sheets can be pulled over each other to create patterns.

It may take several days for paste-paper to dry due to the thickness of paste but the result is worth the wait.

Boxes

A gift box is wonderful for packaging difficult-to-wrap presents. Make your own box from cardboard, use balsa boxes (available from craft and decorator stores), or recycle soap or chocolate boxes.

Adapted from "Beautiful Boxes", written by Judy Newman and published by Sally Milner Publishing, (02) 555 7899, rrp $24.95. Photography by Rodney Weidland

Recycled Boxes

Cardboard boxes (soap, chocolate, or
  any kind of sturdy packaging box)
Paper
Cord or ribbon
Spray adhesive or glue stick
Brass corners (optional)

Cut pieces of paper so that they cover
each piece of the box (ie. lid or base)
plus an extra 10mm on all sides.

Glue appropriate piece of paper to
each box piece so that 10mm of paper
hangs free at each edge. At each corner,
use scissors to clip out paper squares
from paper allowances. Glue and fold
paper to the other side of box piece or
onto adjoining box piece.

Cover each piece in this way, ensur-
ing that any allowances showing on the
box are underneath the base or on the
inside of the box and lid. If the box has
glued tabs, it can be opened out and
glued flat against the paper then folded
and glued together again.

Add brass corners, cord and ribbon
as desired, using the picture as a guide.

LEFT: Recycled Boxes.
BELOW: Torn Tissue Paper Box.
RIGHT: Beribboned Boxes.

Torn Tissue Paper Box

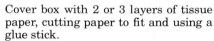

Cardboard box
Heavy cardboard
Tissue paper (3 or 4 colours)
Spray glue or glue stick
Tape

Cover box with 2 or 3 layers of tissue
paper, cutting paper to fit and using a
glue stick.

To make flower pattern, tear petal
shapes of tissue paper along the grain
of the paper. (To find the grain, tear the
paper one way, then the other; it will
tear easily in one direction and this is
along the grain.) Practise until you
have a number of petals in various sizes
and colours and arrange them into a
flower shape. Use the picture as a
guide.

When you are satisfied with the
flower, use a glue stick to glue the petals in place, positioning the darker
colours first, then overlaying the
lighter colours of tissue.

Beribboned Boxes

*These are wonderful containers for
presents of homemade shortbread or
chocolates.*

Set of balsa boxes (various sizes,
  available from craft and decorator
  stores)
Tartan, red and green ribbon
  (different widths)
Craft glue

Glue lengths of ribbon around the
boxes and their lids: wide ribbon on the
box and narrow ribbon on the lid.

Tie ribbon bows (we used double ribbon) and glue them onto the side or top
of each box.

STITCHES

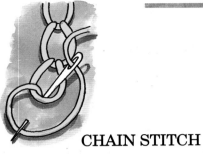

CHAIN STITCH

CROSS-STITCH

Work one half of each cross-stitch in a row, then return and complete the remaining half. Ensure the upper half of all stitches lies in the same direction.

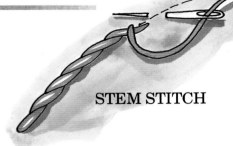

STEM STITCH

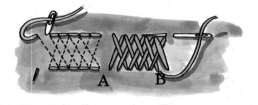

SHADOW WORK

Work a row of closed herringbone stitches from either the right side (A) or the wrong side of fabric (B).

SATIN STITCH

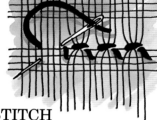

HEMSTITCH

Draw out the required number of threads. Bring out working thread 2 threads down from drawn threads. Take needle behind 4 threads, then around same 4 threads, coming out 2 threads down.

BUTTONHOLE STITCH LOOP

Take 2 or 3 stitches as long as desired loop. Work buttonhole stitch over the threads without catching the fabric.

FRENCH KNOTS

STAR STITCH

Work straight stitches into a central point. Stitches can be the same or varied lengths.

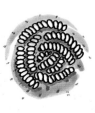

BULLION STITCH AND GRUB ROSE

Bring the needle up at A, down at B and up at A again, leaving needle in fabric. Wind thread around needle point 6 to 8 times. Pull needle through fabric and thread, keeping thread twists in place. Position twists toward B and insert needle. Arrange a group of bullion stitches to make a grub rose.

LAZY DAISY STITCH

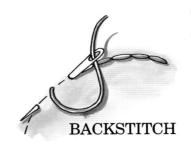

BACKSTITCH

STRAIGHT STITCH

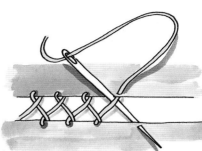

TRELLIS STITCH

Tack two pieces of fabric to paper, leaving space between them. Stitch fabric edges together as shown.

WOOL ROSE

Work a block of 4 satin stitches for rose centre. Work stem stitches around the centre block, curving them and keeping tension loose.

GENERAL INSTRUCTIONS

MAKING AND STITCHING PIPING

1. Fold bias over cord. Using a zipper foot, stitch next to cord.

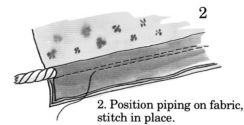

2. Position piping on fabric, stitch in place.

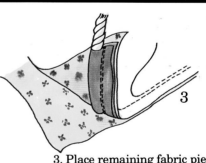

3. Place remaining fabric piece in position, stitch seam.

MAKING AND ATTACHING BIAS BINDING

1. Fold fabric so lengthwise grain and crosswise grain align (bias is at 45 degree angle to both lengthwise and crosswise grain). Cut bias fabric strips desired width.

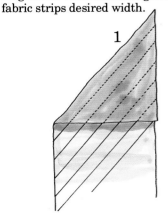

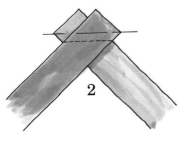

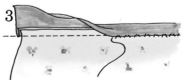

3. Bind fabric edge by aligning raw edges of bias strip and fabric. Stitch and turn binding over fabric edge. Turn under raw edge of binding and handstitch into stitching line, or (4) machine stitch next to binding edge.

2. Join strips to give desired bias length by stitching across straight grain. Trim next to stitching. Press a hem on each side of bias strip and press strip in half lengthwise.

ENLARGING PATTERNS

Patterns which need to be enlarged show a grid of squares with a scale of 1 square = 5cm. This means that each square, when enlarged, should measure 5cm by 5cm.

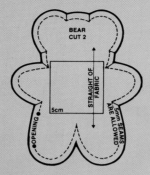

To make an actual size pattern, take a large sheet of paper and draw a grid of 5cm squares, ruling the same number of squares as shown over the original pattern. Copy the original pattern onto paper, drawing one square at a time.

Check the new pattern, making sure it is the same as the original.

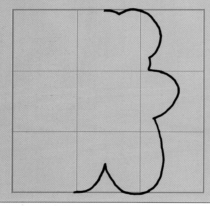

Cup and Spoon Measurements

All spoon measurements are level.

To ensure accuracy in your recipes use the standard metric measuring equipment approved by Standards Australia:
(a) 250 millilitre cup for measuring liquids. A litre jug *(capacity 4 cups)* is also available.
(b) a graduated set of four cups – measuring 1 cup, half, third and quarter cup – for items such as flour, sugar, etc. When measuring in these fractional cups, level off at the brim.
(c) a graduated set of four spoons: tablespoon *(20 millilitre liquid capacity)*, teaspoon *(5 millilitre)*, half and quarter teaspoons. The Australian, British and American teaspoon each has 5ml capacity.

Approximate cup and spoon conversion chart

Australian	American & British
1 cup	1¼ cups
¾ cup	1 cup
⅔ cup	¾ cup
½ cup	⅔ cup
⅓ cup	½ cup
¼ cup	⅓ cup
2 tablespoons	¼ cup
1 tablespoon	3 teaspoons

Note: *NZ, USA and UK all use 15ml tablespoons.*

Oven Temperatures

Electric	C°	F°
Very slow	120	250
Slow	150	300
Moderately slow	160-180	325-350
Moderate	180-200	375-400
Moderately hot	210-230	425-450
Hot	240-250	475-500
Very hot	260	525-550

Gas		
Very slow	120	250
Slow	150	300
Moderately slow	160	325
Moderate	180	350
Moderately hot	190	375
Hot	200	400
Very hot	230	450

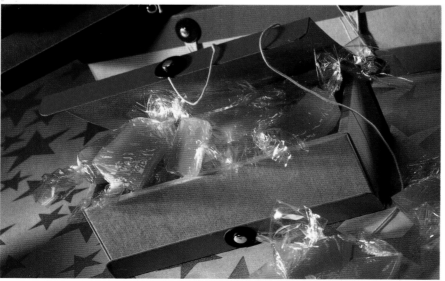

ABOVE: Butterscotch.

INDEX

BACK COVER: Background: Do-It-Yourself Wrapping Paper, page 120. Top left: Fresh Herb Wreath, page 67. Top right: Avocado Body Cream, page 49. Centre: Economical Wraps, page 115. Bottom left: Pistachio Turkish Delight, page 75. Bottom right: Shortbread, page 86.